PRAISE FOR *THE FAMILY GUIDE TO AGING PARENTS*

"*The Family Guide to Aging Parents* is a helpful and practical resource for family caregivers and professionals. Written by an experienced geriatric nurse and elder-law attorney, it offers useful health care and legal information and I recommend it for students, professionals, and the many families grappling with these challenging issues."

—GARY SMALL, MD, Author, Professor of Psychiatry and Aging, Director of the Longevity Center at UCLA

"Carolyn Rosenblatt has written a crucial guidebook for the millions of Americans who are dealing with the unfamiliar challenge of helping aging parents live safely and with dignity. Through a combination of practical tips and instructive true-life stories gathered during her years as a nurse, lawyer, and now family mediator, Carolyn provides smart advice on everything from getting Dad to give up the car keys, to talking to parents about their finances, to protecting them from elder abuse."

—JANET NOVACK, Personal Finance Editor & Washington Bureau Chief, *Forbes Media*

"My suggestion to patients, families and loved ones is this: when you find a reliable source of information, buy it, use it, share it, and keep it handy. This book is a timely and powerful information source to fill a need as to where to go and get help. Knowledge is power. This book is a source of power for Americans as we age ourselves and assist our loved ones."

—ELAINE G. SWENSON, MPH, BSN, RN

"Ms. Rosenblatt's *Family Guide to Aging Parents* brings great insight and deep personal caring to matters concerning the elderly. She has extensive background in difficult elder law matters including dementia, elder abuse, and fighting amongst family members, and I have worked with her on several of these. She is able to apply her experience and compassion from her work as a registered nurse to her practical book."

—ELIOT M. LIPPMAN, ESQ., elder law attorney

THE FAMILY GUIDE
TO AGING
PARENTS

Published by Familius LLC, www.familius.com
Familius books are available at special discounts for bulk purchases for sales promotions or for family or corporate use. Special editions, including person-alized covers, excerpts of existing books, or books with corporate logos, can be created in large quantities for special needs. For more information, contact Premium Sales at 559-876-2170 or email specialmarkets@familius.com

Library of Congress Catalog-in-Publication Data
2014959238

Paperback ISBN 978-1-939629-57-9
Hardcover 978-1-942672-73-9
Ebook ISBN 978-1-942672-00-5

Printed in the United States of America

Edited by Michele Robbins and Lindsay Sandberg
Cover Design by David Miles
Book Design by Brooke Jorden

10 9 8 7 6 5 4 3 2 1

First Edition

THE FAMILY GUIDE

TO AGING

PARENTS

Answers to Your Legal, Financial,
and Healthcare Questions

CAROLYN ROSENBLATT, RN, ELDER LAW ATTORNEY

*This book is dedicated to the memory of my grand-mother, **Louise Blondeau Crum**, a remarkably intelligent, kind, and supportive influence in my life. She was my saving grace many times over, and her guidance and support got me through so many difficult times. She aged well and was fully engaged in her community until she stopped driving in her eighties. She was an RN, and I am sure that was a big reason why I decided to become a nurse. Influenced by my grandmother, I have loved working with older people since I was a child. Her legacy has inspired me to help others.*

ACKNOWLEDGMENTS

No book comes to life without the help and input of others. For me, a lot of technical help came from my loving husband of thirty-two years, Dr. Mikol Davis—my partner, my IT guy, and my friend. He offered his wisdom, perspective, and help with all things. If my computer froze or I couldn't find the draft, he was there to retrieve it, bless him. If I wanted a psychologist's perspective, he gave it. I owe him a great deal in bringing this book to life.

In addition, I sincerely thank Ben Bernstein, PhD, psychologist, performance coach, and author of *The Workbook for Test Success*. He suggested connecting with Familius, our publisher for this book. Without him, I would not have known about them and their many contributions to families everywhere.

Finally, I acknowledge the countless clients who have sought my advice and counsel, pouring out their hearts and sharing their difficulties and successes with me. Each of you has taught me so much. I have taken some of your stories and woven them into this work, hoping that what you have taught me will, in turn, help others get through their challenges with greater confidence.

CONTENTS

INTRODUCTION

This book came to be as a result of a transition. My own personal and professional changes were the motivations that caused me to want to write the book.

After I had worked as a nurse and then as a lawyer, I transitioned out of law practice to become a mediator and consultant. The consulting work began to occupy a larger part of my time. I noticed that many of the clients I saw with aging parents had similar problems. The questions began to reveal certain themes: Worries about finances, relationships, and where and how to best care for aging loved ones. There were issues about older parents reluctant to give up driving, despite the safety issues their adult children saw. Clients asked what their legal obligations were to their parents and what their parents' legal rights were, especially to refuse help. Adult children were overwhelmed with the extensive amount of information on the Internet, from legal sites to caregiver sites to questions about how to pay for care. Seeing these trends, I thought it would be good to write down some of the things clients and I talked over.

My husband, Mikol Davis, a clinical psychologist and my partner at AgingParents.com, encouraged me to put my answers to client questions in writing. Often, he and I worked together, particularly with clients who were in the midst of family conflict. His insights and forty years of professional experience in providing mental health services were and continue to be invaluable in assisting adult children to solve their problems and meet their challenges with aging loved ones and with siblings. His input was also helpful when the person seeking advice was the elder. Together, we came up with more ideas and suggestions than either of us could have done alone. And, as it happens after thirty-two years of marriage, we work well together.

I also recognized that some prospective clients could not afford private consultations about their loved ones or family issues. I wanted to make as much basic information available to them as I could, without their having to pay attorneys' fees for consultations. So, Mikol and I talked it over, and I began to write. From time to time I asked for his advice about many of the issues I address in this book. It truly is a combination of healthcare, legal, and emotional health advice for families with aging loved ones. The first edition of this book came out in 2008. As time went by, I learned a lot more about client stories and about writing itself. I had become a blogger by 2010, and writing for *Forbes.com* also taught me a great deal about those who were in the reading audience, as comments on various posts came in. When I found out about Familius as a possible publisher for an improved edition of my writing, I knew it was a good fit.

You will see a strong message throughout this book to plan ahead to avoid some of the worst outcomes I have seen with adult children and aging parents. No one needs more stress in life, and planning can help you avoid it.

The book is designed for you to use a chapter at a time, if you have a particular challenge in your life that corresponds to a chapter title. However, if you want general overall preparation for addressing the legal, financial, and health care needs of an aging loved one, the entire book can help you. Though each chapter can stand on its own, all of the subjects I address are interrelated, and sometimes all these issues I discuss affect the same family within a short time. For instance, an elder who has memory loss issues may need help at home, may be unable to manage finances or drive any longer, and will need someone to have the legal authority to make decisions about money for her. I walk you through how to work through all of these issues and more.

I especially want any of you who have siblings and aging loved ones to focus on the potential issues with family disputes in the chapter devoted to family conflicts. These conflicts are a significant difficulty for many, since some families just don't get along very well. I am hoping that my advice will save some heartache for anyone who has to face these painful family fights. There is a path to peace.

Finding that path starts with having the essential conversations with your aging loved ones and family members.

Another significant thing I suggest repeatedly throughout the book is to do your research. I give you plenty of direction about what to look for and where to find it. You will likely find additional resources of your own, since the number of sites designed to help with issues concerning aging is increasing steadily as our population ages. Take time to research and explore your options when any change is needed for your aging parent, such as moving, applying for public benefits, or choosing a helper for the home. This will help you make an informed choice as a consumer.

Most importantly, I urge you not to just read and think about these subjects. There is a clear need for you to *take action*. Don't wait for your parents to get old or for there to be a right time to act—this is not something anyone should put off. The time is now. If there is a single point I can make, it is that you need to get moving to plan for your aging parents and other elder loved ones.

As you read through any part of this book, picture me and Mikol being there for you as you consider our advice. It comes from the heart and from a genuine desire to help you avoid things that trip people up in the changes brought on by aging parents. Imagine yourself feeling much more confident from reading this book as you try your best to be helpful, and to do the right thing. It can be really hard, but it's worth the effort. We stand with you.

WHAT YOU NEED TO KNOW ABOUT

FINANCES

AND AGING LOVED ONES

One of the biggest mistakes we adult children make with aging parents and other loved ones is the failure to talk about finances. We may be lulled into a false sense of security, thinking that our parents have always been independent and that we don't need to worry. Or, we don't like to talk about subjects that are just plain uncomfortable.

But as our population ages and people live longer than ever before, we must prepare for new challenges as adult children of our elders. We have to address the issue of how our aging parents are going to manage as they live into their eighties, nineties, and beyond.

Will they run out of money? Some do.

Will they be able to make safe decisions? Some cannot.

The purpose of this chapter is to introduce a few of the subjects about finances that we see come up quite often. Since we usually have no formal education for how to deal with aging parents and the finances that support them, most of us are unprepared to take on the discussion of finances with aging parents, much less the responsibility of having to help support them if we ever need to do so.

For many, our aging loved ones may have survived the Great Depression, leaving them with an emotional response to talking about money. They might feel that it's too private; it's none of your business; it's not polite; or you don't need to worry about it—they're fine. That resistance often shuts down conversation, and we adult children (and sometimes spouses) are left in the dark. In this chapter, I hope to shed some light on things every family needs to know about, and I encourage you to bring these things up with your aging loved ones—both for your own sake and for theirs.

AGING AND FINANCIAL DECISIONS

The problems of aging are both physical and mental. Time can erode our mother's or father's alertness, memory, concentration, and decision-making capacity. And while memory loss and confusion may not seem to interfere too much with life at first, they can each affect financial decisions. Dementias, including Alzheimer's disease, slowly, but surely, damage mental capacity. The capacity for safe financial decision-making will erode over time for anyone with dementia. Our loved one's decision-making capacity is typically not lost overnight, except in cases of sudden, catastrophic change, such as stroke, head injury, or the like. In most instances, the loss of ability is gradual, and we can see it progressing over time. We must pay attention to the signs which indicate that our loved one can't handle the checkbook any longer. These can include noticing collection letters in your parents' home, seeing that they have paid a bill twice or not at all, finding out that a utility has been cut off due to an overdue payment, or finding out that an insurance policy has been cancelled due to failure to make a premium payment. These signs can also include your aging loved one giving checks to any solicitor who asks for money, whether by mail or on the phone. The only way to find out about these situations is to check. You will need to look for these things when you see your loved ones.

No one likes the thought of losing independence. We tend to avoid talking about the possibility of this happening to us. We put it off. Then time goes by, other concerns come up, we get distracted by them, and we may not remember that memory problems can destroy the ability to understand the legal documents that will eventually protect our loved ones in their later years.

The following story is an example. The names are changed to protect the identities of the people involved.

Mary, Marlene, and Their Stepdad, George

Mary and Marlene are sisters, three years apart. Both work full time. Mary is single, and Marlene has a husband and two grown children. When they lost their mother to cancer five years before their current situation arose, they became even closer to their stepfather, George. He had been married to their mom for over twenty years, and they loved him. He was always kind and generous to them. He had been successful in business and owned a large home where the girls had spent part of their growing years. He was in good health, but a year after his wife passed away, he began to have memory problems and had to retire.

George was typically very responsible about his legal matters. He had a will. He had a trust. He had a lawyer whom the sisters both knew, since he had been doing George's legal work for some time. However, George stubbornly refused to finish all the legal paperwork the lawyer wanted him to sign. One of those things was a Durable Power of Attorney, appointing Marlene, the older sister, to be in charge of his finances if he were ever disabled and needed someone to take over managing them. George never signed it, and his lawyer never pushed it. Marlene and Mary asked him about it once or twice, and he said he'd get around to it. But, he never did.

As time passed, George began to suffer worse memory

loss and have a lot of physical health problems, too. He was diagnosed with dementia. Mary and Marlene were his only family members nearby, and they arranged for caregivers to come in and help him every day as he became increasingly frail. George could still sign checks, but he really didn't know what he was signing.

The cost of the caregivers began to eat away at all of George's savings. His income wasn't much, but he had a good nest egg in his retirement account. When the sisters saw that he was low on funds, they realized they would need to tap into George's retirement income to pay for his caregivers.

They contacted the financial institution where his retirement account was maintained, but no one would talk to them. They had no legal authority to even ask what was in the account.

"Do you have a signed and notarized Power of Attorney?" the manager asked. Since neither sister did, they were stuck.

At that point, and because they were not going to be able to pay the caregivers, Marlene and Mary had no choice but to contact an attorney to find out what they could do. That was an expense they had not planned on for George. George's former lawyer had no signed Durable Power of Attorney, and the girls were upset with him for not doing what they thought was his job. The new lawyer advised that, since George was not competent enough to understand anything about his finances and could not make decisions anymore, their only choice was to go to court and have George placed under guardianship (called conservatorship in California).

Some doctor's reports, a few thousand dollars, and a lot of time later, the court granted the guardianship and appointed Marlene as the guardian over her stepdad. She could then get the funds in George's retirement account and continue to pay for the caregivers.

What George Could Have Done to Save Thousands of Dollars

In this case, the problem was threefold. First, George's lawyer should have been more insistent that he complete his estate planning and sign the Durable Power of Attorney, appointing his stepdaughter to do the job of managing money if he couldn't. No one knew that he was going to develop dementia. But even when he was diagnosed with it, George was still capable of understanding what he was signing. His lawyer did not take action, and then it was too late.

The other part of the problem was George himself. He refused to consider that most of us are going to need help at some time in the future, and we need to plan for that help. He was probably fearful of the idea of losing control over the money he had worked all his life to earn, and that was why he wouldn't sign the Durable Power of Attorney. It turned out to be an expensive choice.

Finally, Mary and Marlene had an opportunity to persuade George to sign the necessary legal document, but they backed away from the subject the first time or two that he refused to discuss it. He put them off until it was too late, but they could have persisted and gotten it done. He loved them and probably would have signed it to please them if they had pushed the matter. Like most adult children, they didn't want to start telling their parent what he was supposed to do, because it didn't feel comfortable. However, looking back on their situation, they both expressed regret that they had failed to get George to give them the document they would need if something went wrong. It ended up causing a great deal of stress, a lot of embarrassment when they could not access his retirement funds to take care of him, and thousands of dollars in attorney's fees to pay for getting the guardianship.

Here is one important thing to learn from Mary and Marlene's story: You don't have to have a lawyer to get a Durable Power of Attorney signed by your loved one. It is a good idea to have legal advice on this subject, and, as a lawyer, I certainly recommend it. But if hiring a lawyer is a barrier to getting the document signed, there are ways to do it yourself, which I will discuss below. It is better to have a do-it-yourself version when you really need it, rather than nothing.

WHAT IS A DURABLE POWER OF ATTORNEY?

A Durable Power of Attorney for Finances is a document that is essentially an agreement that the elder (or other person) signs and has notarized, which appoints an individual, called the agent, to act on behalf of the one who signed the document. This is used when someone is unable to manage finances and other business for himself. The agent must agree to serve in that capacity. Some such documents are valid at the time of signing them. Others require that a physician, or perhaps two, verify that the elder is no longer able to handle finances without help before the agent can step in.

With or without a lawyer, it is legally valid to have the elder sign a Durable Power of Attorney document only while the elder is mentally able to understand what she is signing and doing. A perfect memory is not required, nor is it necessary that the elder have perfect mental ability. The elder who is about to sign such a document must understand what she is doing, as well as the consequences of losing independence with money and other aspects of financial well-being. The elder must be sure that she wants to appoint a person to be the agent to make financial decisions and take over money management in the event of incapacity. She should trust the agent fully, because the agent has the opportunity to misuse such an appointment. It is important for those who have responsibility for the elder to get this document prepared at a time when it is still clear that the elder can make sense of it. Otherwise, it is not legally valid.

When Is It Too Late to Sign a Legal Document?

Deciding when an elder is too impaired to sign a document appointing someone to be the agent on the Durable Power of Attorney is not an easy judgment to make. Many elders with dementia appear physically well, and they may be able to carry on a seemingly normal conversation. However, they may, at the same time, be very impaired when it comes to financial judgment. There is good research[1] to suggest that even in the early stages of Alzheimer's disease, for example, a person may be unable to exercise good judgment concerning money. The ability to make safe financial decisions may be one of the first things to be damaged with the development of Alzheimer's disease and other dementias.

If you are not sure if the elder in your life is capable of signing such a document, ask his doctor to evaluate him for this purpose. The surest way to get a reliable evaluation is to enlist a mental health professional who is trained to assess older persons on the question of mental capacity. A licensed psychologist, neuropsychologist, neurologist, or psychiatrist has the proper training to do this kind of assessment.

Legal advice to prepare the Durable Power of Attorney (DPOA) document is also very helpful because having a Durable Power of Attorney has such an impact on the elder's rights. Properly used, a DPOA is a wonderful tool that allows a loving relative to help a vulnerable elder manage his assets and do business safely and legally. Wrongly used, it is a license to steal. Because of the risk of signing power of attorney over to someone who might abuse the position, every elder should have this important document ready before it is too late. It is too late when the elder can no longer think straight or make good decisions. People may reach that point at different times, or not at all. There is no exact age when it should be done. Consult with your parent's doctor to ensure your elder is prepared and protected, particularly if there is any question of memory loss, early dementia, or other concerns about your loved one's capacity for financial decisions.

Undue Influence

As people age and begin to have cognitive decline, they may lose their ability to see that someone is trying to take advantage of them. This makes it easy for others to use the opportunity to get an aging parent to do things that are not in the elder's best interest. Most often, family members are in a position to exert this kind of power over a vulnerable person. We call the concept "undue influence."

One does not have to be cognitively impaired to be a victim of undue influence. A person can be manipulated even when she does not have any cognitive problems. It is a matter of the trust she has in the one manipulating her that causes her to be gullible, suggestible, and readily taken advantage of by the manipulator.

The legal concept of undue influence varies in different states. Generally, it refers to a person in a trusted position using that position to get an older person to act in a way that is not in the elder's best interests. In many states, the law protects elders from being manipulated by those who abuse their position of trust with the elder by imposing legal consequences for undue influence.

When an elder is dependent on another person, such as a relative, a caregiver, or a financial advisor, that person is in a position to exert undue influence to get the elder to benefit the person upon whom the elder depends, usually by getting the elder to give him money or sign things that can cause harm to the elder.

Here is an example:

Maura's Case

Maura, age eighty, had been in a successful business with her husband for decades. She handled all the bookkeeping for the business, and her husband did sales. After he died, she began to have some problems with her memory and keeping track of money. She had only one son, James. Through her Durable Power of Attorney, James was made her agent and trustee when Maura became unable to manage her finances any longer.

Then Maura had a fall and went to the hospital. After Maura was released from the hospital, she needed to stay with someone while she recuperated. Her niece, Susie, who lived several hours away, offered to take her in for the period of recuperation. Maura loved her niece, and James thought it would be fine for a short time. But this niece had always taken advantage of Maura's generosity.

Maura went to Susie's apartment to recuperate, and James did not hear from either of them. He started calling, and when he did, he became alarmed. Susie had not been giving good care to Maura, who had not left the apartment since arriving there two weeks before. James also found out that Maura had been making large cash withdrawals from her account, which was very unusual. James questioned Susie about this, and Susie hung up on him.

James contacted an attorney and began to look into the matter. This caused a huge rift in the family, but James was still very concerned. The next thing they knew, Maura had signed a new Durable Power of Attorney appointing Susie as the agent. Two lawyers were now involved in a case in which James' attorney claimed that Susie had used undue influence to get Maura to appoint Susie as the agent over Maura's funds so that Susie could benefit.

This was clearly a case of undue influence. Maura trusted her only son, James, to look out for her best interests and to watch her finances, but when Susie had Maura in a dependent position, Susie convinced Maura to change the Power of Attorney. This was not for Maura's benefit. Worse yet, Susie did everything she could to turn her aunt against James, saying that he was trying to steal from Maura.

The issue of undue influence is widespread. Aging persons who depend on others are vulnerable. A problem with the Durable Power of Attorney is that a person can be talked into changing it later. Many dollars in attorney's fees were spent by James, and Susie, using Maura's money, to try to defend what Susie had done. Maura was easily manipulated by Susie.

The lesson here is that a frail elder can be subject to manipulation. Her funds can be diverted for the benefit of someone else, she can be talked into signing things that only benefit the manipulator, and, in extreme cases, the elder can be left destitute. If your aging parent has appointed you as an agent on the Power of Attorney document and they begin to have cognitive problems, it is time to pay close attention to who is around them and what changes are taking place. In James' situation, he felt somewhat uncomfortable with Maura going to stay with Susie, but he let it go. That was a point at which he needed to communicate with Susie what the rules were about Maura's finances. He had complete control over them at that time. He might have communicated the fact that he was paying close attention to what Susie was doing, and that well could have stopped her manipulation before it got to the point of possible abuse and the need for attorneys.

James could have removed most of Maura's money

from her checking account before Susie had a chance to get her hands on Maura and manipulate her. In that kind of case, the new account can be in the name of the agent only. If Susie didn't like it, she would have had to go to a lawyer to try to get access. Having a lawyer involved can help, since the lawyer is ethically bound to avoid harming a vulnerable elder in this situation, even if she is hired to represent the Susies of the world. In Maura's case, a licensed fiduciary was eventually appointed to oversee all spending of Maura's funds. With that supervision, it is not likely that Susie would be allowed to buy herself a house with Maura's money when Maura needed it to pay for her own long-term care.

How Do You Get a Durable Power of Attorney Document?

An estate planning or elder law attorney is the usual one to prepare the document. Signing a Durable Power of Attorney is part of a good estate plan and is often done in connection with setting up a trust, writing a will, and getting a healthcare directive signed.

If your aging loved one does not have a Durable Power of Attorney and does not want to pay a lawyer, the forms can be found on the Internet at no charge. Search for "durable power of attorney" for your state, since the language varies from state to state. Even with variations, this kind of document is valid outside the state where it is signed, provided all of that state's legal requirements to make it valid are met. The signature must be notarized by a notary public, but one does not have to go to court or have an attorney create the document.

The advantage of doing it yourself is that you save money.

The disadvantage is that the person appointed as the agent may not fully understand the legal obligations of being the agent.

Legal advice may be needed to ensure that the obligations of the agent are clear and that the person signing the document understands how serious it is. Conceivably, the person signing the Durable Power of Attorney could change his mind and appoint different people as time goes by. This can cause a great deal of conflict and can easily lead to abuse, as we saw in Maura's case. A lawyer can help the person doing the appointing to make a good choice of agent and can provide guidance to the agent as well.

At this time, courts are not at all involved in supervising the agents who serve in the role of power of attorney. No one needs to know who is appointed, and it could be done secretly. The disadvantage of no court involvement is that no one is watching what the agent or person with power over another's finances is doing. There is a risk of financial harm to a partially competent or incompetent elder.

When Is the Right Time to Ask a Parent to Sign a Power of Attorney?

It is appropriate to ask a parent whether he or she has signed a Durable Power of Attorney at any time while the parent is still capable. The subject needs to be part of a series of discussions about the future and what might happen if a parent became incapable of managing independently.

Someone must take the lead. Often, it is the most capable adult child among siblings. Whoever takes the lead explains that the whole family needs to take some time to have these discussions. There are many issues parents face in planning for the future. All adult children need to be part of the planning.

It can be a very difficult subject to bring up with an aging person. Loss of the ability to manage finances properly does not necessarily mean that the elder is completely out of it. Many older persons are very reluctant to face the possibility of health decline or to admit to changes in their independence with anything. Bringing up the subject gradually and with numerous discussions over time can make it easier for all to handle.

IF YOU ARE APPOINTED AS AGENT ON A DURABLE POWER OF ATTORNEY, WHEN SHOULD YOU TAKE OVER THE FINANCES?

There is no simple answer to when to start with your duties as agent for an aging parent. The document may have been prepared years or decades before it becomes necessary to use it. However, if your aging loved one is over age seventy-five, you know that there are more risks of memory problems at that age than there are with a younger person. Memory problems are an early warning sign that dementia may be developing. Many people who have memory loss do go on to develop dementia. By age eighty-five, at least a third of the population has dementia. What is very clear is that people with dementia should not be left to their own devices in handling money, regardless of how educated, smart, or experienced they have been with financial matters.

Take a look at your loved one's finances and see if there are irregularities or inconsistencies. Talk with family members and determine if your parent is starting to slip in his financial judgment.

Dementia

For the purposes of this discussion, I use the word *dementia* interchangeably with Alzheimer's disease. Dementia is actually a symptom of the disease, with Alzheimer's being the most common cause.

Dementia is a slow and tragic brain disease that robs a person of the ability to think clearly, to reason, and to remember, among other things. It is different for each person. However, everyone with dementia of any kind will suffer from loss of the ability to think clearly and to make safe judgments.

If you have an aging loved one who is showing signs of memory loss, such as not being able to keep track of a conversation, forgetting what happened a few minutes ago, or repeating himself a lot, then it is definitely time to watch over the finances. He could be developing dementia, though you cannot automatically assume that's the case. Memory loss is often a sign of the impairment that leads to dementia.

What to Do First If Your Loved One Is Becoming Forgetful

One of the first steps to take is to have a discussion with your loved one about what you see. This must be done gently and respectfully. It will probably seem threatening to the person who has the symptoms, since she is likely terrified to be losing control. You might ask if your aging parent has had any trouble remembering the bills or the checkbook balance. If your parent is willing to admit it, that gives you an opportunity to offer to keep track of things for her.

A next step is to be sure that the banking records are kept online. Whether or not your aging parent uses a computer, you need access to the account information online so that you can track how well your parent is doing, and most importantly, whether there is anything irregular going on.

Finally, it is very important to review an aging parent's will and trust if she has one. If there is a trust, the trust will specify who should take over for the aging parent when she becomes impaired. There is no standard way that trusts are written. The language surrounding what triggers the need for a successor to take over varies depending on the lawyer who drafted the trust.

Some trusts say that the elder has to have two doctors declare that he is incompetent for finances before a successor can assume responsibility. Some trusts say one doctor is enough. Others are written more liberally, and a mental health provider is specified as the one to make the decision about an elder's lack of competency for financial decisions. Generally, the area of deciding financial capacity for decisions is very difficult. One important point to understand, though, is that financial capacity is a legal determination, rather than a medical one. The lawyers depend on healthcare providers to give them necessary information, but if there is a dispute about it, a lawyer and sometimes a judge decides.

Alice's Story

At the time of this writing, my mother-in-law, Alice, is ninety-two years old, and she lives alone. She had never done online banking in her life until age eighty-six. Her husband died, and she had to learn a lot about using a computer, as well as paying her bills. Unlike most eighty-six-year-olds, she did learn, and her son, my husband, Mikol, was not only able to teach her, but was also able to add his name to the accounts, so that he could monitor her activity. Mikol and I have worked together to help Alice as needed, though she is still quite independent.

Mikol had to get a power of attorney from her banks so that he could communicate with them and transfer funds as needed if she were unable to do so. This gives her peace of mind and gives her son assurance that no one is taking advantage of her. Mikol checks her online bank statements every month, and, if there are any questions, he discusses them with her. Fortunately, she does not resist this assistance; rather, she is glad he is checking on her finances. Alice does not have memory loss, fortunately. If she did, we would have needed to monitor her bank activity even more closely. Perhaps we would be paying her bills for her by now. We know that everything is in place in case Alice ever did need more extensive help.

It must be noted here that Mikol already had a Durable Power of Attorney, appointing him as Alice's agent. However, the bank wanted its own Power of Attorney form filled out by Alice, since it would not accept the standard, state approved form. This can be an issue for you if you are to be the agent on a parent's DPOA. Be sure to get a similar form from any bank where your loved one has an account, and have your parent also sign the bank's form for POA. If the time comes that you need to assert your authority as the agent, the bank is likely to insist on this. Although you could probably win a legal fight about it with the bank, it is simpler to just have your aging parent sign the bank's form for POA, as well as the standard form your state offers to anyone an elder wants to appoint to serve in this capacity.

Currently, Alice is protected from any irregular activity by our monitoring of what comes into and goes out of her accounts. Mikol's oversight of her finances extends to her investments as well. As agent and power of attorney, he is added to her brokerage account, too. He gets brokerage account statements every month and reviews them.

We saw the benefit of this arrangement when Alice had a different financial advisor. She was sold an inappropriate investment by that advisor. Mikol found the problem. After some research, we found that government regulators are now prosecuting advisors and brokers who sell such things to elders. Mikol contacted the advisor by mail and demanded a refund of the amount invested. The advisor, with some difficulty, finally did refund all of the money invested in this unsuitable product.

Getting online access to account records enables the agent to move money out of an account and away from an elder who is subject to manipulation. But if the elder is able to do his normal activities, he may not even notice that he is being protected by a loved one. The advantage of keeping some of an elder's assets in a separate account, which the power of attorney agent can do, is that it prevents the elder with memory loss or poor money judgment from being scammed or taken advantage of by a predatory person.

This is another example of how vulnerable elders can be, and Alice has no dementia. Imagine if your loved one did. There are far too many people in our world who want to take advantage of an aging, vulnerable person.

What Can You Do If a Parent Resists Talking About Finances?

There are certainly many aging parents who do not want to talk about their money. They may fear that someone will take advantage of them if they reveal what they have.

They may be embarrassed at having so little left.

They may feel it's impolite for you to ask.

They may fear that you will take their independence from them.

No matter the reason behind the resistance, it is important to recognize that finances can be quite an emotional subject. Approach it with respect and clearly reassure your loved one that you are concerned, that time is going by, and that the conversation needs to take place.

If you pitch the subject as necessary because of your concerns about your aging parent, you may get further than if you suggest it's for your parent's own good. That is one possible way into the conversation. Most parents do not want to be a burden to their children. Help them realize that you need to discuss finances for *your* sake. Without having the essential information, you are going to feel stuck and helpless. You will be burdened by not having any information.

If your aging parent resists, you will need to keep trying until you get what you need. Sometimes bringing in allies can help. Trusted other older relatives, another sibling, clergy, or the parent's attorney all could be sources of help. Whatever it takes to persuade your loved one to help you get the basic financial information you need must be done. You don't want to end up like Mary and Marlene—having to go to court for a guardianship or conservatorship because you don't have a signature and your elder is no longer capable of signing anything. You do not want to have to go through additional hardship because you do not know where to find essential financial information.

There may be some elders who will not give you any information you need and will not sign a Durable Power of Attorney. If there is a family trust as part of the estate plan, these individuals refuse to step down as the person in charge. They will not see a doctor to be evaluated. No one can move forward to protect them. These same individuals are truly a danger to themselves because they do not recognize that they are impaired.

Sometimes, in the worst cases, you do end up needing to use the courts. When a parent has failed to appoint anyone as an agent to serve as power of attorney and then loses his ability to understand or sign a document, you are left with no choice. The court will need to hear evidence and make a decision as to whether a guardianship or conservatorship is needed.

THE PROBLEM OF DENIAL

Occasionally, an elder will request help from a trusted other person when she or he senses that she or he is not able to handle money any longer. However, it is more common for the elder to resist allowing this kind of help.

Imagine never being able to write a check again and never being able to freely choose how to spend money without having to have someone overseeing you. It is not surprising that this entire subject is fraught with difficulty. Money is very symbolic of independence for most people, and loss of independence can be upsetting, depressing, and threatening for an elder. Loss of control over money can symbolize loss of control over life and loss of freedom.

Even though the subject is difficult, it is critical to be on the alert for common danger signs that an elder is slipping and needs someone to step in and take over the finances.

If you are the agent on a Durable Power of Attorney document, or you are appointed as a successor trustee on your parent's trust, you have a duty to watch out for your loved ones. You will need to get a sense of when it is time to step in. If both parents are living, this can be harder than if you have just one left. When memory loss creeps in, the less impaired or unimpaired parent often covers for the one who is losing memory.

Denial: Gina's Story

An eighty-three-year-old client, Gina, was in my office to discuss signing a Durable Power of Attorney appointing her daughter as her agent. This daughter had contacted me because her father had recently been hospitalized. She described how her father had dementia, but everyone, including her mother, just kept acting as if he were fine. He had become violent one day and had struck Gina. She was already recovering from surgery and could only walk with a walker when her demented husband hit her. She had to call Adult Protective Services to come to her home. They called the police, and her husband was taken to a nursing home for care, probably for good.

Gina was vulnerable, too. The couple had made their own will, but neither had signed a Durable Power of Attorney. Gina was feeling as if this were a nightmare. She told me, in tears, that just a month ago her husband was still driving his car. She had been afraid he might have an outburst. She saw his behavior getting worse and more unstable over time. She said, "You see the changes, right in front of you, but you don't want to face them. They're in front of your nose. You know it's wrong, but you just don't do anything! And then something like this happens, and you wonder, why did you wait until it got so bad?"

Gina is a perfect example of how human it is to not want to face the painful and tragic things that can happen with dementia. Gina is fortunate that she was not hurt beyond a few bruises when she was struck by her husband. He did not know what he was doing. During the entire time he had been developing dementia, he had also been handling the family finances (however badly), and no one had insisted that he sign the necessary documents to allow his daughters to step in and assist with their financial matters.

Gina knew that her husband was in a dangerous state, but had great difficulty bringing herself to contact anyone outside the family for help. Finally, he was taken away in a crisis. There are many families who face this issue of increasingly difficult behavior, but they feel fearful and do not act until an extreme situation forces a change. Gina's husband had always been in charge. He was slipping badly, but no one wanted to confront it. No one wanted to say, "Please stop. I'll take over the bill paying now." My message is to please not let it get that far before you step in to help. It will save grief, aggravation, embarrassment, and even possible physical harm if you act rather than wait too long.

The worst thing about waiting too long to get a document signed, or even to discuss financial issues with your aging parents, is that you always think you have more time. No one can guarantee that, of course, so it is prudent to put it on your calendar to bring it up at a specific time and date and get past the procrastination that affects so many adult children.

Warning Signs That It Is Time to Step In and Help with Finances

As we have discussed, the effects of memory loss, confusion, and dementia can creep up slowly. The signs may be very subtle at first. As financial judgment is likely to be among the first abilities to erode, adult children may be fooled into thinking that things are fine. Socially, the parent may seem able to participate. He may seem to be doing things as usual, until you look more closely. There are always warning signs of trouble. You are well served if you know what the red flags are.

Red Flags That Indicate Your Elder Needs Help Handling Money:

1. The elder has forgotten to pay an important bill and you notice collection letters in the elder's mail, or bill collectors call on the phone when you visit.

2. The elder has neglected a part of daily life, which she or he has always attended to in the past. Forgetting housekeeping, neglecting personal grooming, not

maintaining the yard, not putting gas in the car, or other forms of forgetting can alert you to the fact that something has changed.

3. The elder forgets that you were coming to visit, even though you called with a reminder just before arriving. This is an indicator of memory loss—don't dismiss it.

4. The elder exhibits marked weight gain or loss, which can be a sign of depression or other mental or physical health problems.

5. The elder is spending money on things he or she does not need and normally would not want. Odd-appearing changes in spending habits can be a sign of loss of ability to make safe decisions.

6. The elder is getting telephone calls and items in the mail asking for money, and he or she is inclined to write a check or give money to all of them.

7. The elder gives personal information to strangers on the telephone or at the door, sometimes including bank accounts or credit card information.

8. The elder has made a new "friend" who calls or visits often, and who, you find out, has persuaded the elder to give money to him.

9. The elder is isolated, has limited transportation, and has a lack of social networks from which to draw companionship.

10. The elder has recently lost a spouse.

All of these warning signs can suggest that the elder is vulnerable to financial loss or abuse. Any one of them suggests that your loved one is at higher risk than before for making mistakes, being swindled, or becoming a victim in some other way. It is necessary to attend to any of these warning signs and act quickly. Financial abuse of elders is ruthless, shocking, and prevalent. The fastest and least expensive way to protect your impaired aging loved one is to take over handling all finances for him under the legal permission of the DPOA.

USING FIDUCIARIES TO HANDLE FINANCES FOR AN ELDER

When an aging person does not want family to take over handling the finances, but may be willing to allow someone else to do so, one option is to hire a professional, called a fiduciary. Fiduciaries are licensed in some states. They are qualified to take over financial management when there is mistrust between an impaired elder and the family members, or among the family members in charge who cannot agree or do not trust each other.

A fiduciary can be an attorney, an accountant, a bookkeeper, or anyone who is qualified and capable to do the job. It is safest to hire a fiduciary who has a license to serve as such or who has some other license demonstrating knowledge and skill, such as a retired CPA. He or she will have enormous power, so it is critical to choose very carefully by checking credentials and references. The fiduciary gets the authority to serve as manager of the elder's finances by having the elder assign the fiduciary the responsibility of agent on the Durable Power of Attorney. If a family member is already appointed, but doesn't want to or can't serve as the agent, then a family member in authority can appoint a fiduciary.

THE LAST RESORT: GUARDIANSHIP

When an elder is in danger of being taken advantage of or is being manipulated, has no DPOA, and nothing else works, it may be time to use the law to protect the elder. Guardianship is typically an expensive process that involves hiring an attorney to represent the person(s) who thinks the elder needs to be under guardianship. The elder will also have an attorney, sometimes one appointed by the court to represent his interests or to defend against the effort to get a guardianship. For your loved one, it can be a very traumatic experience to appear in public court and hear all manner of testimony about how he is impaired. It can pit one family member against another and damage or destroy family relationships. That is why I suggest it only as a last resort.

Once a court decides to grant the request for a guardianship, the person appointed to serve as the guardian (or conservator) has the responsibility of keeping track of every penny spent for the elder and must periodically provide a written account to the court. The decisions about how to spend an elder's money and keep careful written records can be burdensome. The guardian has many decisions and duties on top of the necessary accounting. It is a difficult job.

A great deal of what is ultimately accomplished by a guardianship can be done with the Durable Power of Attorney, which is why I encourage everyone to use a DPOA whenever possible. A DPOA can be very helpful to keep the process of financial management for an impaired person simpler, less expensive, and easier on the agent than guardianship.

HOW TO AVOID COURT: MEDIATION

If your aging loved one is willing to talk about finances with a neutral person, then that is a possible way to avoid a guardianship or conservatorship. A neutral, trained professional can assist the family in working on a solution. We call this mediation. It requires bringing in a mediator who works with families to see if an agreement can be worked out. It is a very cost effective way to avoid going to court, but it also means that all involved must buy into the idea. Mediation is a voluntary process. There is great value in using a non-relative to offer a perspective to the family from the outside looking in. Sometimes, the neutral mediator can help the elder hear the concerns of the family better and feel less threatened, since a good mediator will always be sure that every person at mediation has a chance to be fully heard.

Mediation is not just a conversation with an outsider. It is a process that takes knowledge of conflict resolution principles and techniques to help the parties reach their own resolution. One of the greatest advantages is that it is private and allows unlimited creativity to craft an agreement about what should be done. It is also far less expensive than hiring lawyers and going to court, where there is far less opportunity to work things out as the family wants them worked out.

SUMMARY

Aging can take a toll on anyone's ability to manage finances safely. Because we have such a widespread problem of elder financial abuse, we all need to be aware that our aging loved ones are at risk. Every family needs to discuss the real possibility that at some time an aging loved one may lose capacity to make independent financial decisions. Because it is so important, I encourage you to have a signed and notarized Durable Power of Attorney completed for your loved one. It is never too early to do it, but it certainly can end up being too late to get it when you need to protect your aging parent.

THE PATH TO
PEACE
IN FAMILY ARGUMENTS ABOUT AGING PARENTS

This chapter digs into an everyday problem that affects most families. Sure, there are lots of families that get along very well. But there are plenty of families we've encountered who don't get along, and sometimes siblings refuse to even speak to each other. Then, suddenly, a crisis forces them together to share the tasks of caring for an aging parent or making decisions about an aging parent. What should be done then?

My experience and that of my husband, clinical psychologist Dr. Mikol Davis, are combined here to offer tips and insights into the problems families face with their aging parents. Sibling warfare or arguments between elders and their adult children can be very painful. Often, siblings and family members in this conflict avoid fighting by avoiding those family members, but an aging parent's change in condition or health issue forces them to communicate. If their patterns of communication have been historically dysfunctional, these patterns re-emerge in the context of dealing with aging loved ones. Most people seem lost and don't know how to structure better ways to communicate.

We encounter this situation often and have worked as mediators and advisors with many families in conflict. We share this experience with you here, offering you insights gained from families who have succeeded in solving these arguments and those who have not succeeded. We can learn from both.

FREQUENT SOURCES OF CONFLICT

One of the biggest problems we see is the unrealistic expectation that somehow a sibling who has never taken much responsibility for Mom or Dad in the past will change and begin doing so now, because help is needed. We have seen a pattern that responsible ones in a family tend to continue to be responsible when care for aging parents is needed, and irresponsible ones tend to continue to be irresponsible.

Caring for aging parents presents a huge challenge for their adult children, especially when those parents suffer from declining health problems over a long period of time. The burden on caregivers is significant. It can bring out the best and the worst in a family. Consider what happens as a health concern that may start out with helping your loved one a few times a month evolves into a daily responsibility. Since families rarely anticipate long-term care, they may have unrealistic expectations about how much help will be needed over time. These unrealistic expectations can lead to resentment toward siblings who may do less than others in the family.

And added to the stress of the caregiver is the problem that those who live far away from an aging parent will likely have a different perspective from the one or ones who live close by and therefore see the changes in a parent much more fully. This gap in understanding lies at the heart of many disputes.

Another issue that triggers resentment and arguments is the uneven distribution of work and financial responsibility that falls on some family members, as compared with other family members. Some siblings are better equipped, both emotionally and financially, to step in when a parent needs help. Some are simply unwilling to share the load. Others take on responsibility at great personal sacrifice. We often see the failure to discuss how to make the workload fair among those capable of helping the aging loved one.

Those responsible for aging loved ones may be in the "sandwich generation," caught between responsibility for their own children and the responsibility of taking care of their elders. Some have teenagers at home and are dealing with the issues of adolescence, while simultaneously managing the changing needs of a declining parent. Others are middle-aged parents of adult children themselves, working and trying to manage the growing needs of their aging loved ones.

Some adult children are at retirement age themselves, hoping for some enjoyable time after their working years. They find themselves saddled with unanticipated responsibility for an aging parent or in-law, and their plans are severely altered. Others are the only child, responsible for both aging parents. These situations are stressful. They add to the difficulty of the caregiving itself.

In addition, people are living longer with all the care and treatment available for conditions that used to leave us with shorter lives. What some may have expected to be a few months of caring for an elder can turn into years. We have few role models from prior generations who lived as long as our parents may live. And yet, as overall longevity in our country increases, the caregiving period adult children undertake may be much longer than we plan for and much longer than we can easily afford. Some gerontologists advise us that we are likely to spend more years caring for aging parents than we did raising our children.

Elders with difficult personalities or cognitive problems add yet another layer of difficulty to family dynamics in caregiving. We have little to guide us in knowing what to expect. Yet many people do take on the care of aging loved ones willingly and with good intention. As they find themselves in unexpected, challenging, and long, drawn out situations, there is sometimes a feeling of panic, rage, or helplessness.

Sometimes sibling conflicts are a result of geography: One adult child lives near the aging parent, and the other(s) live out of the area. The adult child nearby is somewhat required to take care of things, simply because she is close by. This can lead to resentment on the part of the one who must "do it all." Even for those who willingly take on the many tasks of managing the care of an aging parent until the end of life, it is inevitable that caregivers will feel the burden. Depression is quite common among adult children who take care of their parents. The job is demanding and stressful. Physical and mental decline in a parent can cause enormous emotional upheaval in the adult child who watches the parent's strength, vitality, and mental faculties ebb away.

Relationships become strained.

Marriages become strained.

The burden and financial needs of parents who have low income can create guilt, fear, and a sense of being overwhelmed in any adult child facing these issues.

The Only Child's Unique Conflicts and Finding Resources

Sometimes even when there is no conflict with siblings, there can be conflict with other relatives. An aunt, uncle, or someone who has been close to your parent can cause just as much trouble for you with decision making as a sibling. Even the family physician may disagree with you about whether to resuscitate your parent or to treat an illness when your parent is elderly and frail. Even disagreement between two doctors caring for your parent(s) can be a source of stress.

Conflict with others who may not agree with your decisions is better handled if you have taken the time to examine your own feelings and reactions to the decision-making process. There is value in consulting with another person, especially if you are an only child, and it can balance the human tendency to respond primarily from our own fears while making decisions that affect others' lives. It is difficult to be objective about what a parent would want when you are in the middle of the crisis and are also dealing with your own emotions. Now is the time to ask for help and perspective. Even if you are independent, willing to help your aging parents and other relatives, and sure you can handle all this, it cannot hurt to run your thoughts by another person and ask for input. This eases the burden you will inevitably feel in making so many caregiver decisions yourself.

If there is no reliable or helpful trusted person in your life, social networks of caregivers are available and growing. The National Family Caregivers Association, for example, provides support and resources for you, the caregiver, rather than for the aging person. Internet chats, message boards, blogs, and other means of connecting through resources like this give you the opportunity to pour out your worries to others who may be in your situation. Local branches of this and similar organizations conduct meetings, retreats, and support groups for caregivers. All of these resources can be helpful for those who are faced with difficult decisions and feel alone in doing so.

Deepening an Understanding of Sibling Conflicts

Perhaps you never got along with your sister. Maybe you have had no use for your brother in years. Now, suddenly, a crisis forces siblings with old issues between and among them to deal with each other. Old patterns of relating tend to resurface when a parent needs the assistance of adult children. What can one do? What should one expect?

Lifelong behavior patterns will still be there, even when it seems that they *should* have changed. In our work, we see many families in which one or more siblings take the lion's share of the burden of caring for aging parents. About 90 percent of caregivers we encounter are women.

Without speculating as to all the reasons why this may be so, we can look at the statistics and conclude that if you are the daughter, there is a pretty good chance that you will be at least one of the responsible ones caring for an aging parent. Some sons are excellent caregivers and fully devoted to the task, and we see this in our practice, too. But whether you are a son or a daughter of an aging parent, if you have siblings, the primary caregiver sibling may feel that the burden of managing the parent's care falls unfairly on him or her.

Although the work of caregiver can have many noble, beautiful, and even humorous moments, it is also filled with hard physical effort and emotional turmoil. It can lead to angry exchanges between the direct or primary caregiver and the sibling or siblings who are not as involved. Nasty, bitter exchanges of words, telephone calls, or emails can come from the bed of resentment, which could well have remained dormant were it not for the state of Mom's or Dad's health. If you are in this situation with your siblings, what can you do?

The underlying dynamic of these conflicts is often found in expectations. The expectation may sound like this: If our parent needs a lot of care and attention, everyone should step up and share the load. Though this may indeed be a reasonable expectation, it may not be a realistic one. Family members who have historically been responsible will likely continue to be so at the last phase of a parent's life. Those who have not been comfortable with or at least willing to take responsibility for a parent are unlikely to do so at the last phase. Recognize these patterns and adjust your ideas about what other siblings should do. Resentment can be mitigated by changing one's expectations.

It can be very difficult to accept the fact that one person or two in a group of siblings is doing all the work. You may be that person, and it is unfair. It can stay that way for a long time, even for years. However, there is no changing a sibling's character. The primary caregiver(s) can and should ask the available and able siblings to share the work. Stating your needs and expectations clearly and in a non-threatening way is a good start. Most of the time, you can't get what you need without asking for it.

For example, you can say to a sibling, "I'm taking Mom to the doctor twice this week, besides making sure she gets all her medicines every day. Will you help me out by taking her to her appointments next week?"

A direct approach does not work for everyone. Different styles work for different people. The point, though, is to ask for what you need, rather than expect that another sibling will simply step in and help because it should be obvious that help is needed. In many families, it just doesn't work that way. For you in the primary caregiver role, failing to ask for help and silently fuming about not getting help can only lead to angry outbursts, and possibly to depression and resentment. And even when you ask for help, you must be prepared for the possibility that you will not get it.

Middle-aged siblings may have a million excuses for not helping you.

A way to manage your own mental and emotional health is to be prepared not to have help from siblings and to alter your expectations of help if it is not forthcoming. If you can afford to pay for assistance, don't hesitate to get it. We need all the support and assistance we can find with the chores and responsibilities of caring for our aging parents. If funds are limited, you have no choice but to forge ahead and do the work yourself. In that case, enlist the help of friends, churches or synagogues, community agencies, volunteers, and whatever resources you can locate in your area. There is no need to be a martyr and take on the burden alone while resenting deeply that the weight all falls on you. Whatever is available to you should be searched out and tried to reduce your workload as the primary caregiver.

If you are not in the habit of asking for help from others, remember that this is a special exception to what your life was like before. Your parents or other aging relatives will only go down this road once. Without help, you can end up sick yourself, depressed, or unable to help. If you cannot rely on siblings, rely on others who are more willing. Once you reach out, you may be surprised and gratified to learn that many people are kind, generous, and willing to give some time to you and your loved one to make things a little easier. Asking for help from others will do much to alleviate the risk of rage, resentment, and physical upset over siblings who have let you down. Should your parent resist or complain about outsiders coming in to help, point out that the help you have solicited is for you, and that you are doing the best you can.

Controlling Conflict by Communicating in Advance

It is important in a family to quickly identify one sibling who is going to take the leadership role. If you have difficulty identifying who will take that role, then it is necessary to select a leader by volunteering, by rotation, or by election from the others. The person identified must be willing.

The next step is to identify the extent of the needs of the aging loved one. This identification may be very difficult if you are a long-distance caregiver. Even if you live in the same community, it can still be difficult to identify the extent of a parent's needs. We find that this is a daunting job for many families, due to the fact that differing ideas and beliefs among family members about aging can color the process.

Any personal fears, deeply held notions about how things should be, or denial of the parent's decline in health and ability can distort your view of a parent's needs. For example, some people believe that caregiving should be the daughter's responsibility. There are a lot of daughters out there who find this attitude infuriating. They may have perfectly capable brothers whom they see as simply too lazy to do the work. This pattern is likely to create a lot of anger and may damage relationships.

In our practice, we see adult children volunteering for the care of aging parents with a naïve view of the extent of a parent's true level of need. The vision in the adult child's mind of what will be involved turns out to be far less than what actually is needed on a daily basis. Yet, in spite of this, there may be little or no examination of the belief that the daughter should always take on the caregiving. The one on whom expectations are laid may fail to speak up and ask to have a joint conversation with siblings. Instead she just keeps doing the work. Sometimes this has serious emotional and physical health consequences for the primary (or only) caregiver.

Martha and Her Mom

Martha is a sixty-five-year-old retired teacher, who lives across the country from her mother, age eighty-eight. When her mother fell and broke her hip, it became clear that Martha should move her mother to live closer to her. Martha has two sisters who live in different states from Martha. As she was discussing with me what sort of living situation would be best for her mom, she did not anticipate the caregiver issues her mother now presents. Mom is immobile without a walker. She has never lived in Martha's state and has no friends there. She wants her independence, but it is unlikely that she will be able to manage without some supervision.

One mistake Martha is making in the early stages of caregiving is the failure to have a family meeting, even by phone, to talk over all the things that are coming up and must be anticipated as Mom ages even more and likely needs more caregiving. Martha has not asked her sisters to discuss Mom's needs now or how they may evolve in the future. She is taking on the caregiver role with little preparation and an unrealistic view of what is going to be needed. After she moves her mom closer, and as it dawns on her how much work she is taking on by herself, Martha will likely begin to be angry and want her sisters to help out with some of the work.

Martha has not taken a full leadership role in her family by initiating the necessary conversations. She believes that setting up the move and moving Mom nearby is being a leader—and to some extent it is—but we can see that a few months down the road or a year from now, she is likely to wish she had thought ahead. True leadership also involves asking her sisters what they would be willing to do and how they could help relieve her from the constant responsibility she is volunteering to take on. When the work gets heavier, a plan needs to be in place to avoid a fight among the sisters.

Using Resources to Help with Planning

Siblings who are facing new caregiving roles can avoid some family arguments by getting an outside professional to provide an assessment of the aging parent. An objective and qualified person outside the family can help everyone plan realistically about how much care their aging parent needs and how to organize it.

Your area's Agency on Aging is a helpful resource. There is one in every county. The job of these government funded agencies is to connect you with resources in your parent's area. They may refer you to senior services organizations, social workers, public health nurses, or geriatric care managers who can help supply unbiased information. Neutral information can give siblings a basis for planning ahead for caregiving and also for such division of labor as your family can handle and provide.

As an example, Martha, in the example above, could get a referral to a geriatric care manager in the city where she lives via the Agency on Aging. The care manager could recommend suitable living situations for Martha's mother, suggest ways Martha could help provide a good quality of life for her mother, and recommend ways the sisters could share the responsibility. The care manager may suggest that Martha's sisters take turns being available for their mother, so Martha can take breaks or vacations from her caregiving job.

AVOIDING CONFLICT BY GETTING LEGAL DOCUMENTS IN ORDER

Legal documents may not be what you think of when you think about how to ward off a family argument. But, they are very important, since they give legal authority for important decisions to someone other than your parent.

For instance, a Durable Power of Attorney (discussed in the first chapter) is a document that allows the aging parent to appoint an agent to make financial decisions of all kinds on her behalf should she lose capacity to make those decisions. Whether siblings are in accord or not, this DPOA gives full authority to the agent appointed to take over the financial management for an incapacitated person. Although there are risks and benefits to DPOAs, they can avert conflict if the agent is competent and honest, and is acting in the best interest of the impaired person. While the elder is still competent, he makes a choice of whom to appoint with the intention of preventing any argument about who is supposed to be in charge. Giving that legal authority and planning ahead for possible incapacity is a very valuable gift from an aging parent to his children. It can prevent conflict if it is done well. Doing it well includes having a family discussion about the assignment of the agent and initiating the necessary conversations. The person the parent appoints to be the agent on a DPOA should not be a surprise to anyone.

Along with a DPOA, a living will or advance health care directive may fend off or alleviate fighting over a parent's end-of-life treatment. Nearing the end of life is usually a highly emotional and stressful time for everyone. At least, with an advance health care cirective, we know what the elder wants at the end of his life. The benefit of such a document, which everyone should have, is twofold. First, it lets every family member know what to do or not do if the time comes that your loved one is unable to speak or make decisions. Second, it requires that your aging parent pick someone, or more than one person, to be in charge of making health care decisions for him if he is incapacitated. That appointed person has legal authority to decide, even if other family members disagree.

Joe's Advance Health Care Directive

I have seen how the advance health care directive (which is also known as a health care proxy or power of attorney for health care) can help to ensure that your loved one's wishes are carried out. It also helped my family resolve conflict when my father-in-law's wishes were not recognized by his daughter, my sister-in-law. My husband was the only agent on the directive. Years before, he had discussed this with his father, Joe. Joe had originally put both of his children on the directive, which means each had equal veto power over decisions. This could surely lead to conflict. For example, let's say my husband sees the world rather differently from how his sister sees it, and there was an old history of their not getting along. My husband, Mikol, asked his father to choose one of them, not both, to put on the directive. He said that he was fine with letting his sister have the job if it was ever needed, but he did not want to share it with her. He could see how she was likely to let her own emotions get in the way of doing what Joe had said he wanted at the end of life. Mikol did not trust that they would be in harmony or agreement. Joe thought it over and decided to appoint only Mikol.

And, sure enough, at the last part of his life, Joe was in the ICU and unconscious when it came time to make important decisions about end-of-life. Mikol's sister was frantic and extremely emotional, and she wanted every-thing done to keep Joe alive. This was the opposite of what the health care directive said. She had heated words to say to Mikol. In the end, however, after Mikol had thought things through, he was able to remind his sister that Dad had given him the responsibility to make the decisions. Eventually she relented and let him do so. In these instances, the document was helpful in the process of decision-making between siblings, even if the hospital staff seemed to be ignoring it.

Not all families can work out this kind of disagreement by themselves. There are screaming family fights in the hospital corridors over these issues in many institutions. Even where there is a health care directive, the doctors may refrain from taking sides and continue all treatment, despite the health care directive, as they may fear getting sued if they follow the directive and stop care. Mediation can be a great help to families who are in conflict over end-of-life issues.

A WAY TO RESOLVE CONFLICTS ABOUT LEGAL DOCUMENTS

There is an option toward resolution of these issues that many have never thought about and I hope you will now consider. That option is to use a neutral professional to mediate the conflict before it spins out of control and leads to misery for every person involved.

Mediation was introduced as a concept in the prior chapter. Now we explore in greater depth how the mediation process can be used to help resolve family conflicts about any issue they face.

What Is Mediation?

It is a process that uses a neutral person to help both sides of a conflict work out their own solution. The mediator provides guidance, information, and feedback. A mediator can guide a discussion to resolution when the parties are willing to resolve the matter.

As a mediator myself, I am a strong advocate for using this method to find solutions to family disputes. In my practice, mediation has been effective, regardless of the subject, approximately 80 percent of the time.[1] That success rate seems much better than the success rate of siblings at war who try to work out a conflict about a Durable Power of Attorney for Finances or end-of-life wishes in the hallway outside the ICU.

How Does Mediation Work?

Typically, when a situation has reached the point that it does not seem feasible that the people involved can keep a conflict in control, and emotions are high, the siblings or family members have to think about getting someone outside the conflict to help them. Let's say there are four family members in disagreement. Two are on one side of an argument, and two are on the other side. In mediation, all four would have to agree to sit down with a neutral person for the purpose of trying to work out their differences.

The next step is finding a mediator. There are community mediation services all over the United States, particularly in larger cities. Courts frequently use mediators to try to settle cases in hopes of averting trial. Most court cases which go to mediation are settled in mediation. Courts have lists of available local attorneys and other mediators trained in resolving disputes. If you have a case involving a dispute that is already filed in court, the judge may suggest mediation of the case or the lawyers involved may want to mediate it. In those situations, you and your attorney will likely have a list of mediators to choose from. Often lawyers representing the parties already know mediators they trust and will work on finding a mediator all can agree upon.

Paying for Mediation

When a case is not a court matter, anyone is free to find and use a private or volunteer mediator. Mediators list themselves on the Internet and in local directories. While volunteer services are free, private mediators usually charge a fee for their services. You will pay a fee by the hour or by the mediation, but you are more likely to get a private mediator whose experience with conflicts matches your problem than you would find using a volunteer mediation service.

For example, if the dispute involves an elder, you would look for someone who does elder mediation and has training or a background that provides some expertise in this area. If the dispute were about a parent's estate, you would look for someone who has experience in probate law, real estate, family conflicts, or related matters. The mediator's expertise and level of experience is important.

Volunteer mediators often staff community mediation centers. They are likely to be low cost or no cost for low-income clients. You may get lucky and find one who has the skill or background you are looking for. However, a highly skilled mediator may be able to resolve most kinds of conflict, even if she does not have exactly the background that matches your problem. Good mediation is a matter of trusting the mediator to be neutral and accepting the mediator's leadership to help you and your family reach a resolution. If the trust is not there, it will be difficult to accept suggestions or information from a mediator.

Mediators vary in personality and style as much as people in general vary in this regard. Find a mediator that meets your situational needs, as well as your personal needs and style. Before you hire a mediator, research possible mediators, check out any website a mediator has which would highlight his or her background, and ask for a summary of the mediator's experience.

Many mediators are attorneys, though mediation does not require a law degree. Some states require that mediators be certified, and some do not. Mediation skill does require training and experience. If you use a mediator, find the best person you can for the price. Search the Internet, check local directory listings, and ask an attorney—if you know one—who can refer you to a qualified mediator. Mediate.com has listings across the United States. Local mediators may also advertise locally. In the areas of conflict we have been discussing in this chapter, someone who does elder mediation would be a good choice, since the issues are elder specific.

Does the Mediator Decide How the Dispute Should Turn Out?

The mediator does not make any decisions for you. The mediator is not the judge of right or wrong. Rather, the mediator acts as a referee, a go-between, or a person who draws out what people really want in the course of talking about a problem. A mediator asks good questions, listens well, offers suggestions, provides an objective viewpoint, and encourages every person to describe what it is he wants to do to resolve the dispute. She is not in a position, legally or otherwise, to make a ruling on anything, nor to tell anyone what to do. A skilled mediator can do a great deal to help your family find your own way out of a problem by encouraging and helping you to reach the solutions, compromises, and agreements that fit your specific needs.

What Is the Difference Between Mediation and Arbitration?

There is a great deal of difference between mediation and arbitration. Arbitration is a formal process in which a dispute is decided, often in a final way. Arbitration may take the place of a trial in court. It may have lawyers representing each side. The arbitrator is in a position to judge who is right and who is wrong. The arbitrator does make a ruling or decision. The arbitrator acts as a judge. Rules used in court are also used in arbitration.

On the other hand, mediation is a less formal process. If a lawsuit is involved, attorneys will attend the mediation in hopes of getting the case settled. If a lawsuit is not filed, there may not be any lawyers at all. Often in elder mediations, lawyers do not participate, as these generally involve a family member in conflict with another family member, and there is no legal case. Without the formality and rigidity of arbitration, mediation can be very helpful in reducing the anger and fear that often accompany issues with elders in failing health.

You may consider hiring an attorney to help settle a conflict about an elder. The disadvantage of using attorneys at private family mediations is the cost. The participants at mediation are usually paying both their attorneys and the mediator by the hour. It gets quite expensive. Ideally, the family engaged in an emotional struggle and dispute can get it to mediation before lawyers are involved or lawsuits are filed.

SPECIAL CHARACTERISTICS OF PARENT–ADULT CHILD CONFLICTS

It could be that you, as an adult child, disagree with your parents over the idea that they need any help. The conflict may have many causes. Elders of Baby Boomer children are survivors of the Depression. They are socialized to "tough it out," "keep a stiff upper lip," and to try to avoid burdening anyone else. Elders who grew up during this era may not discuss their own feelings much, or at all. They may be very polite and uncomfortable around confrontation. They may not even have the vocabulary to discuss their emotions in any detail. "I'm fine," and "It will be okay," may be as far as communication goes.

Both the culture of being independent and the ingrained habits of not asking for help can truly be sources of conflict when Mom and Dad begin to lose the ability to care for themselves. Fear of loss of control often motivates the refusal of help. Parents simply do not want to face the possibility of dependency, being "put in a home," having to give up their right to handle finances for themselves, or anything else which is seen as a threat to their independence. When well-meaning adult children approach their parents with the prospect of getting help, strong resistance can cause tremendous stress for the adult children.

Often, you breed conflict when you fail to plan in advance with parents who do not like to face the possibility of needing anyone to help them. When there is no advance planning, conflict may be worsened further because siblings may disagree about what to say, what to do, and what is good for their parent.

It's true, though, that some parents simply refuse to plan ahead. Their refusal is probably out of denial that they are getting old and fear of losing independence. It is common, though it is a predictable source of conflict down the road when the reality of losing independence becomes a crisis.

Avoiding Conflict Through Necessary Conversations

If there has been no advance planning, where do you start? If you live in your parents' area, and you have noticed a significant decline in their abilities over time, you are at an advantage. At least you have more frequent contact and a basis for having a conversation with them than those adult children who live at a distance have. If the information your parent gives you about not needing help comes only from talking to him or her on the telephone, you cannot truly know the extent of any problems he or she may have.

Start by making a visit. If it is inconvenient, consider that it will probably be much more inconvenient to get a call in the middle of the night advising you that Mom or

Dad is in the hospital, and you have no idea what to do once you get there. A personal visit gives you an opportunity to bring up the touchy subjects of finances, planning how to pay for any care that becomes necessary, and getting legal documents in order.

The in-person visits and necessary conversations about the future also give you the opportunity to collect essential information. Think of your advance-planning visit as a preventive step to take for your benefit, ease, and sanity. You can avoid arguments with your parents and other family members later if you know what documents exist, where to find them, and what assets your parents have. You will manage any crisis that comes up far better if you know who the doctors are, where the financial documents are kept, what medications your parents take, what kinds of insurance they have, and where the policies are kept.

Even being made aware of the actual state of your parent's health can help avoid conflict. For instance, if you understand that your parent has a chronic health problem that is likely to get worse over time, you can educate other family members and start working on planning ahead. You will not have to feel inept or blame anyone else for not telling you about these issues if you take these steps. If you share all the information with all siblings and other close family, you will likely be able to manage crises with a calm demeanor and less conflict.

Many conflicts are driven by fear or feelings of being disrespected or of being left out. Imagine that your work to get essential information and to have necessary conversations can eliminate some of these risks for those who share responsibility with you. Without the necessary information that planning in advance will yield, your family could be a time bomb for conflict. Avoiding conflict is possible, but it takes effort. Someone must always take the initiative to have the difficult conversation.

If, for example, you say, "Dad, we really need to talk about finances now," and your father refuses, you can say that you need to talk about it tomorrow, and gently insist that you will still be there the next day. You need to bring it up repeatedly on such a visit. In overcoming a parent's resistance to talking about these emotionally laden matters, it is important to dispel the myth that not discussing it will be less burdensome on you, the adult child. You will need to point out respectfully that it will be much worse of a burden on you if the subject is not discussed, because you have no way of knowing how to help your parent in a crisis if the subject is not addressed.

Donna, Pam, and Robbie's Conflict

Donna, her sister Pam, and their younger brother, Robbie, have a father who is ninety-six and living in a skilled nursing facility. He has multiple health issues and can't take care of himself. He appointed Donna to be his agent on the Durable Power of Attorney, and she is also his agent on the health care directive. Donna and Pam live in one state, while Robbie lives in another, and Dad's skilled nursing facility is in yet another state. Dad always paid for Robbie to come and visit, since they enjoy each other's company and Robbie can't afford the travel expenses on his own. Dad is getting low on funds, even though he has long-term care insurance to pay the nursing home bill. Dad had been paying Robbie whatever he said was the cost of travel. It seemed to be very generous, but it was not questioned. No receipts were ever provided. It had been this way for quite some time.

When it became clear that Dad was no longer capable of making financial decisions and he was not going to be in charge of his funds any longer, Donna told Robbie that she had to take over managing the money, and he needed to start accounting exactly for what he was spending to come and visit their father. They had never discussed being accountable before, and that was a mistake.

The result of Donna asking Robbie for receipts and being exact in his accounting was a barrage of ugly emails from Robbie to Donna. This could have been avoided. All three siblings could have had a conversation about Dad's future financial picture, covering these issues: He has lived a long time, and no one expects him to pass away anytime soon as he seems to rally after any health episode. The money in savings will not last forever. All siblings needed to be conscious of dwindling funds and the fact that insurance did not cover all of Dad's expenses.

An essential conversation that should have taken place could have resulted in a yearly travel budget for Robbie and a clear method for keeping track of all expenses going out of Dad's account over the prior two years before things got unpleasant.

During your advance-planning visit with your parent, make notes or record the conversation. Once you have recorded what your parent wants to say, you have a tool available to you that can prevent or at least reduce conflict in the future. Your parent may later experience memory loss, which is increasingly problematic as we grow older. The risk of dementia, and particularly Alzheimer's disease, rises with age. If your parent forgets, you have his own words to remind you and your parent of what he wanted and what was said at a clearer time. The recording of this information can also reduce the risk of sibling conflicts over what Mom or Dad really did want before she or he lost the ability to recall this information.

Necessary Conversation Checklist

Here is an abbreviated list of topics your conversations about finances should cover. These are questions to ask. This will not take place in a single visit, since you will be asking for a significant amount of detailed information. Space it out and cover a few at a time.

1. What is their income, and what are the sources of income?

2. What are their debts, and how are those being paid (include credit card debt, mortgage, loans, etc.)?

3. Where do they keep their bank accounts, investment accounts, and cash? You will need the account numbers and passwords if they bank online.

4. If either or both parents were involved in an accident tomorrow, what financial tasks would need to be accomplished over the next month, and how would those get done?

5. What does it cost them to live each month? Where do they keep copies of their tax returns?

6. What insurance policies do they have? Do they have long-term care insurance, life insurance, and supplemental health insurance? Where are those policies kept?

7. What savings, investments, and other valuable assets do they own? Where are they located? Who has access to them?

8. Have they ever signed a Durable Power of Attorney? Where is it located? Who was appointed agent?

9. Have they done estate planning—getting a will and trust—and if so, who is the attorney who prepared these documents?

As you can see, the financial conversation is more than a single talk. Rather, it is likely to require a series of conversations to get to all of the important and necessary subjects that would allow an adult child to competently take over managing finances for an aging parent.

For those who need a resource to help ensure that the basics are covered, we offer a tool for purchase at AgingParents.com called the Family Security Planner. It gives you organizing sheets with all the topics listed above so that you can ask the right questions and have one place to record the answers. It also gives you a sample (California) Durable Power of Attorney and advance health care directive form.

Getting Help with the Stonewalling Parent

Some parents cannot be convinced by gentle persuasion to discuss subjects such as their finances, their health, or other matters they consider no one else's business. In those situations, it is again time to seek help. The consequences of not doing any advance planning and refusing to let the adult children know where to find the necessary documents and information can be disastrous.

Enormous expenses for attorneys and court proceedings can come from parents' refusal to disclose things a caregiver must know at the time of an emergency. If your parent is willing to let you come along to a doctor visit, that may be a way to get information from the doctor as to what is needed and what medicines your parent requires. If your parent has a lawyer, financial planner, accountant, bookkeeper, financial advisor, stockbroker, clergy person, or other trusted person, it may be easier for your parent to allow you to speak with that individual than for your loved one to talk directly to you. Ask for permission. If your parent does not, for some reason, trust you or your judgment, seek the help of someone the parent does trust. Perhaps there is another relative, a good friend, the parent's sibling, or someone else your loved one respects. Ask for help with this difficult situation.

Someone not emotionally involved is more likely to appreciate the urgent need to get the information for advance planning. *The advance planning information is what is important. Who, in particular, obtains it is less important.* And if the trusted person can make a good recommendation for you, you are ahead of the game in trying to avert the conflicts that come from assumptions and confusion later on.

Finally, it is good to know that so many resources are available to Baby Boomers and their parents for the planning process. Additional information on what to talk about in necessary conversations is listed for you in some of these resources. Checklists of the necessary information everyone needs to get are available, as mentioned, at AgingParents.com, on the Internet, and through attorneys, legal aid offices, senior centers, Agency on Aging offices, social services, and books.

SUMMARY

Conversations about finances are very personal and can be quite difficult for some aging parents. Because of their generational values of privacy concerning money matters and fear of losing control or being taken advantage of by their families, they may strenuously avoid these conversations. The resistance they feel and express can lead their loved ones to back off at the first sign of their unwillingness to discuss the subject.

But procrastination and avoiding the subject of your parents' financial matters can lead to significant distress for you and the family in times of crisis. It can also lead to significant risk to your loved ones as they age and potentially lose the capacity to manage their own financial lives safely. If the aging parent will not bring up the subject, it is up to other family members to do so, even if the parent resists the conversation.

The right questions asked at the right time in a respectful way offer you the best chance for success with this sometimes touchy subject. Persistence must also be a critical part of the adult children's strategy when aging parents are unwilling to talk about it. You must continue your efforts to gain access to essential information if you want to be able to help your aging parents, should they lose their independence. I hope that the examples I've shared with you here about what happens if one procrastinates will offer some inspiration and motivation to get started or to keep moving ahead in your efforts to have these financial conversations.

Recommended Resources

- Carter, Elizabeth, and Monica McGoldrick. *The Family Life Cycle: A Framework For Family Therapy*. New York: Gardner Press, 1980.

- "Elder Mediation: Families at War." *YouTube* video. www.youtube.com/watch?v=DSLx9JwDK-M. Accessed August 4, 2014.

- "Elder Issues Mediator." www.Mediate.com/Eldermediators. Mediate.com. Accessed August 4, 2014.

- "Find an Elder Mediator." www.ElderCareMediators.com/find-an-elder-mediator. Mediate.com. Accessed August 4, 2014.

AGING PARENTS AND GIVING UP
DRIVING

A group of Sun City senior citizens was sitting around talking about their ailments:

"My arms are so weak I can barely hold a cup of coffee," said one.

"Yes, I know. My cataracts are so bad I can't even see my coffee," replied another.

"I can't turn my head because of the arthritis in my neck," said a third, to which several nodded in agreement.

"My blood pressure pills make me dizzy," another went on.

"I guess that's the price we pay for getting old," winced an old man as he shook his head.

Then there was a short moment of silence.

"Well, it's not that bad," said one woman cheerfully. "Thank God, we can all still drive!"

When we learn to drive, the driver's education course never tells us how long we're safe to drive. Community programs for older driver safety do emphasize keeping older people safer by updating their driving skills and providing refresher information about safe driving. But no one gives us a clear idea of the end point for safe driving.

This chapter is for those adult children who believe that Mom or Dad, or perhaps a grandparent, has become a dangerous driver. If you're not sure how to tackle the subject, I hope you'll find some solutions here. If you've already tried to talk about it and been rejected, this chapter is for you.

I urge you to take action if you already know your aging loved one is not safe behind the wheel. Other people need you to do this before something terrible happens. There are many ways to go about approaching the subject of taking away the car keys. This chapter offers my own personal plan to make the job easier. It's based on years of representing victims of accidents, some caused by older drivers who never should have been allowed behind the wheel. When it comes to deciding if the dangerous aging person is okay to drive, please consider it your responsibility. The world will thank you.

WHEN DOES AN ELDERLY DRIVER BECOME DANGEROUS?

No one wants to think about getting old, much less having to give up driving. If you have an aging loved one and are worried about his safety when he gets behind the wheel, you may feel hesitant. Should you bring it up? What if your loved one gets mad? This is such a personal issue.

Planning what to do is a process, and it should never be taken lightly. The impact of losing the ability and right to drive can be very devastating and life changing.

Addressing the subject of whether or not your aging loved one should give up the car keys is tricky at best and emotionally harrowing at worst. A few open-minded and flexible people actually choose to give up driving on their own without being asked. However, many aging adults who become impaired drivers do not recognize it themselves. It's only human for them to avoid the subject or deny it if it is pointed out.

All of us love freedom and independence, and the car is symbolic of total freedom. No one wants to lose freedom, so we can expect that our elders will cling fast to the idea that they are just fine, regardless of what anyone else thinks. Control is very important to our sense of independence, and as people age, the issue of control can become a source of anxiety and fear. Loss of control of anything that symbolizes independence can be a "hot button" issue, and the right to drive is near the top of the list of things over which a person would not want to lose control.

The subject of older drivers and safety is one with which I have extensive personal experience. For nearly three decades, I handled hundreds of injury cases, representing victims who were injured in auto accidents. In cases where the accident was caused by an elder who likely should not have been driving, the situation was usually the same. The elder had no recollection of the accident or did not know what happened. This occurred even when both vehicles were destroyed beyond repair in the collision, the elder had run someone off the road, had run a red light, or caused another such memorable crash.

In one case, the elder had rear-ended the victim and pushed her car off the road and into a tree; he testified that the other driver had come at him and backed her car into his. Of course, this was impossible, given the position in which the police found both cars. His front bumper was smashed into her rear bumper, and she was pinned to the tree by his car. The elder was so confused he literally did not know what he had done. Being confronted with the circumstances of the accident, as happened in a lawsuit, was just too much to face. He could not confront the fact that his driving had caused a crash, so he invented a bizarre explanation.

For aging persons with impaired thinking, this is not an unusual scenario. Memory lapses, slowed reaction time, vision trouble, hearing loss, confusion, and other age-related thinking problems all contribute to the dangers of some elder drivers being on the road. News reports around the country of multiple deaths caused by an unsafe, older driver are sobering. In one such news report, an elder driver stepped on the gas instead of the brake, causing death and injuries. In his confusion, he stated that he lost control of the car for reasons unknown. There is always something that cannot be explained, because the driver is unable to say what happened.

A 2006 study by the Insurance Institute for Highway Safety found that only teen drivers have a higher rate of fatal crashes than drivers age sixty-five and over, based on number of miles driven. In 2003, eighty-six-year-old George Weller killed ten people and injured sixty-three others at a street market in Southern California, driving through "road closed" signs and wooden barriers. He showed no remorse when sentenced to five years' probation on ten counts of vehicular manslaughter. Driving tragedies involving dangerous older drivers, resulting in injury or death, could be a risk for one of your own parents. The injured or killed could be your family members.

Some older drivers are perfectly safe. They drive safely well into their eighties, or even nineties and beyond. Getting older does not automatically mean that one is an unsafe driver, since each person ages differently, and many older drivers with long years of driving experience manage well behind the wheel and are more careful than younger drivers. However, not all older drivers are so lucky as to drive safely until the end of their days. According to the Insurance Institute for Highway Safety, there is a sharp increase in accidents for those drivers who are eighty and older.

Because the subject of whether or not an aging loved one should be driving is often so emotionally charged, people avoid talking about it. They don't want to be the one to bring it up. They fear that their loved one will get depressed, angry, upset with them, or refuse to talk to them. Their fears are well founded. Elders may indeed get depressed, angry, and upset, or refuse to discuss the subject. However, the responsible adult child must step up and deal with this matter when the elder can't or won't.

If you just avoid it, every person walking on the street and every driver on the road is put at risk. If reluctance and discomfort are the worst things you could feel in discussing your elder's dangerous driving, please consider the worst thing the victim or victim's family could feel: grief that their own family member died or was hurt because someone failed to take the car keys away from the elder who should not be driving.

Another consideration is the safety of your loved one. A little confusion or forgetting is a red flag that your elder could have the beginnings of memory loss problems, cognitive impairment, or dementia. Here's an example from my own community. I found this heartbreaking story in my local newspaper.

Dad Got Lost

A middle-aged daughter had a ritual with her ninety-year-old father. Every week they would meet at the same restaurant and have dinner together. The dad was living in a seniors' community, a few miles away, but was able to take care of himself. At his age, he may have had the beginnings of memory problems, but his daughter either didn't notice or was in denial. They loved their weekly dinners, to which Dad drove himself every week.

One rainy night, she had dinner with him, and he left after a nice evening to drive home. He was in the habit of calling her after he got home. He didn't call. She got worried and went looking for him. No sign of her father. Notices went out, and the police did a search. Nothing was found.

The daughter was interviewed. She thought her father may have had a "moment of confusion" and gotten lost. He was never seen again.

This story illustrates that both father and daughter were in denial. Would you think it safe to allow a 90-year-old man to drive alone at night in a rainstorm? If he had a "moment of confusion," it was probably not the first time, and it was probably not a moment. Confusion comes with dementia, as well as some other medical conditions. It is a tragedy that this daughter did not see her father to a normal end of his life and will never know what happened.

WHOSE RESPONSIBILITY IS IT? (WHY DO I HAVE TO DO IT?)

Often, the aging person does not want to face the subject of forgetfulness, much less impaired driving. It is the responsibility of the caregiving family, or the adult children of an elder who is clearly impaired, to look for any signs of memory loss or confusion and take preventive action when the time comes. Getting lost, even one time, going to a familiar place like home is a huge red flag that something is wrong.

Leaving it entirely up to the elder to decide when to give up the car keys is not a safe choice. It may be too difficult for aging persons to be that honest with themselves about their impaired driving. Worse yet, they may not actually realize how unsafe they have become behind the wheel and will be shocked or surprised to hear it.

Memory difficulty and thinking difficulty can happen to anyone. Sadly, elders who suffer from these problems can be so affected by them that they are no longer capable of clear judgment about their ability to drive safely. They may truly believe that their driving is just fine. You, the family member, have to take responsibility, because the elder may simply be unable to do so.

SEE FOR YOURSELF—IS YOUR AGING LOVED ONE SAFE ON THE ROAD?

You may never be able to really know if your aging loved one is safe on the road unless you get in the car with her and observe her driving. If you have reason to think there may be a problem, do not take her word for it that everything is all right behind the wheel. Lack of awareness can arise from a variety of sources besides dementia. Medications can cloud judgment or cause drowsiness; small strokes can impair reaction time and vision; and memory loss may cause your elder to forget about the fender bender or near accident of last week.

We encourage you to assess your aging loved one's situation to determine the risk level. There are various evaluation checklists available. One good example of a tool we suggest is the Texas Aging Network Senior Driving Assessment checklist, available online at TexasAgingNetwork.com and in Appendix A of this book. The checklist helps you, the concerned child, to systematically evaluate the driving performance of your parent. Other checklists are available from insurance companies and local programs designed to improve the driving skills of older drivers. Community-based safe driver programs for older drivers have tools to evaluate driving skills. The local department of vehicle licensing near your elder may have a course and evaluation available.

You will need to set aside time to accompany your aging loved one in the car and be free of distractions so you can watch everything your elder does while driving. Sit in the passenger seat with your checklist. Be honest with your loved one that you just need assurance that she is fine to drive.

Ideally, one should ride along several times at different times of the day to get a thorough idea of what the elder is actually doing behind the wheel. However, one can sometimes get enough "fear factor" in one trip to be convinced that the time has come for the elder to stop driving. If you think this ride-along assessment sounds too formal and structured, just think about how formal and structured it might feel to be interviewed by the police after your elder crashes into something, hurts someone, or worse. Possibly, with that picture in mind, you might feel motivated to overcome your own reluctance to tackle this difficult, but necessary, chore.

If your loved one does just fine when you ride along in the car at different times of the day and night, you do not need to take further steps at this time. However, a repeat of the ride-along should be done every few months. The fact is we all decline in one way or another with age, and the physical and mental faculties we need to be good drivers may also decline. If your aging loved one is not driving well on the ride-along, do not wait to bring up the subject.

You could simply say, "Dad, I'm a little worried about you after driving with you. I think it's time to get a checkup from the doctor to see if everything is okay."

Getting a physical checkup is crucial to determining an elder's ability to drive safely. The medical doctor may see and know things about your loved one's condition that you never knew. The physician can be a great help to you in broaching the subject of whether the elder should stop driving. You will need to accompany your loved one to the doctor or get his or her permission to talk with the doctor.

If you meet resistance from your loved one, you can and should write the doctor a short, respectfully worded letter, detailing your observations from driving with your loved one, voicing your safety concern about your elder's driving, and asking the physician for help. If your loved one's car is banged up, take photos. If there are traffic violations, make copies and include them. Help the MD rely on evidence, so the doctor can make a reasonable conclusion. Enlist the help of other family members or friends, if possible, and add their names to the letter to the physician. The physician may need this, since she is not likely to be in the car with her patient to see for herself. There are physicians who are willing to state that a person who has dementia should stop driving and will tell their patient this directly. Others are less willing for various reasons of their own, sometimes not wanting to alienate a long time patient.

The physician is in a powerful position, because the doctor's word can be much like an order to a state's department of motor vehicles when a person suffers from a risk to driving with a condition such as epilepsy. If a doctor says a person with epilepsy should not drive because he might have a seizure, the state will suspend the patient's driving privileges. No re-testing of the driver is required. It is not quite the same with dementia, which is not as clear-cut as a seizure disorder like epilepsy, but a doctor's role can still be very helpful when the doctor is aware that a person with dementia should not be driving. The American Medical Association asks that all its members inquire about their older patient's ability to drive, though we have seen that this recommendation or requirement is apparently not followed universally. Some doctors are reluctant to get involved in the issue. Others are willing to contact the state department of motor vehicles and either send a form requesting that the driver be re-tested or supply information that the driver should not be driving any longer.

If the driver is unable to pass the re-examination, which means behind-the-wheel testing as well as paper-and-pencil testing, the driver's license will be suspended.

You may think it's the elder's problem, and if he wants to take chances with his own safety, it's up to him—yet it isn't. Every day that passes with a dangerous driver on the road is a day of risk for himself as well as everyone else.

If you have your doubts about your aging loved one's driving, and he is willing to let an objective person evaluate his driving, there are professionals who can do this. Occupational therapy driving specialists can provide a thorough evaluation of driving skills and abilities and do training to keep an older driver safe. These individuals are skilled in counseling and in educating elders about alternatives to driving, should it be found that your aging loved one is just not trainable any further. A statewide list of occupational therapists available to evaluate and train older drivers is located online at 1.AOTA.org/driver_search/index.aspx.

Further, new measurement tools for evaluating visual driving acuity are available online. Objective measurements and evaluations can be helpful if your elder is suspicious of your motives and doesn't trust your assessment of his driving capabilities from having you ride along.

LIMITED DRIVING MAY BE THE FIRST STEP

There may be stages of declining driving ability in which the older driver is still safe, with certain restrictions. For example, since vision usually decreases with age, particularly night vision, an elder may be willing to avoid driving at night. Reaction time to driving situations also slows with aging, and your elder may agree to avoid freeway driving, driving in heavy traffic, or driving to unfamiliar places. You have a better chance with self-imposed restrictions on driving, with the elder's agreement, than if you attempt to dictate them to the elder. These restrictions may enable the elder to keep the car keys longer. However, the burden may fall on the family members to increase the frequency of elder driving observation, since it is clear that a process is underway once any restriction is in place.

As an example, my mother-in-law decided to limit her night driving when she was about 88. She had a scary experience, and she used her common sense to decide that it was too hard to see the road at night, so she just stopped night driving on her own. Many of her elderly friends had done the same.

It is difficult to know when an elder starts to decline with driving and how fast the process of decline will go, so it is up to loved ones to keep watch and protect the elder and others. You can only do this by increasing the amount of knowledge you have about the elder's driving through seeing it directly or getting a formal assessment. If you live at a distance from your aging loved one, you may need to make more visits. If that is not possible, you may need to enlist the help of a friend, neighbor, or other contact who lives near your loved one to do the observing for you. Monitoring an elder's ability to drive on an ongoing basis is a safety issue for the elder as well as everyone else.

Making Agreements

It can be very helpful to look for a way to make agreements with the elder about limiting his driving. If a change in physical status has occurred, such as a fall, a stroke, an illness, a broken bone, or anything that changes mental alertness, it is a good time to bring up the subject of driving and whether it should stop.

Medications and combinations of medications can have side effects which are clear impediments to driving. The starting of a new medication may give you the opening you need to bring up the subject of limiting driving. A medication itself may be the thing that causes a safety problem with driving. The elder's physician or pharmacist can help you find out about side effects of any new prescription or the effects of drug combinations your elder must take. You will need to ask. Many medical conditions and pharmaceuticals can affect the ability to drive safely.

For many people, there is no single incident that paves the way to this subject. Rather, there is a gradual decline in the elder's alertness, memory, physical stamina, vision, hearing, strength, ability to concentrate, reaction time, or any other ability necessary for safe driving. Over time, we start to notice these gradual changes. There may be no event that makes it suddenly clear that there is a problem with driving.

If your aging loved one is willing to make agreements to limit driving, it is a fine first step. Asking for an agreement to limit driving allows a reasonable elder to choose to go along and to maintain a sense of control. Some lawyers advocate getting the elder to appoint someone in the family or a trusted younger person to be the agent who will decide for the elder when it is time to give up the keys. It is much like appointing a power of attorney for making health care decisions. The agent may have only symbolic authority, but the process of writing out a document appointing the agent may do much to ease the decision-making process when the time comes for an aging loved one to stop driving.

WHEN CAN I BRING UP THE SUBJECT?

The aging person is not likely to invite you to start the conversation about driving. Don't expect to hear, "Hey kids, I think I'm a lousy driver. How 'bout taking the keys?" If you wait for Dad to initiate this, you will likely wait forever. If you know there is a problem with his driving, plan what to do. Pick a time—after a birthday, new medication, trip to the hospital, or other major event that reminds us of our mortality may be a good time to discuss the subject. People can be more amenable at such times to facing what no one likes to face, which is that we may be losing some of our abilities.

If you know it is time to address the problem driver, and a family gathering or holiday get-together is planned, ask the family to set aside an extra day or time after the gathering to discuss matters. If you anticipate that your elder may be difficult, strategize with other family members about the best approach. Some conversations may start with such statements as, "Mom, now that you've had a stroke, we're not sure you can manage the car as well as you did before. I'd like to go with you for a ride to see if we need to make any adjustments with your driving."

Resistance might be addressed with statements such as, "I really need you to do this for me, for my peace of mind." If you are able to enlist the help of the elder's physician, you can use factual information, such as, "Dr. Jones says the stroke affected your vision, and we're worried about you not seeing someone coming at you in the car." The American Medical Association has adopted the explicit position that dealing with elders' driving issues should be a normal part of the basic physical and mental exam the doctor does for the patient. Your loved one's doctor may already have questioned her about her driving. If you raise the subject with the doctor, then the physician can provide a source of support and an authoritative voice on the matter.

SIGNS OF TROUBLE

If you notice dents in the car, paint scraped off, or other evidence of minor collisions, you might approach the subject with something like this, "Grandma, we noticed the fender on your car was smashed, and it hasn't been fixed. We'd like to help you. Was there an accident? Can we talk about it?" That may be a way to open the conversation about driving with Grandma in as non-threatening a way as possible.

As with any difficult subject, it will be necessary to bring the subject up respectfully, asking the elder's permission to talk about her driving. If the elder refuses to discuss it, you may try again later, within a short time frame. If that is not possible, because you or others you want with you are not available later, you might insist gently, "We have to do this now, because I have to leave tomorrow." If you keep your tone even, your manner kind, and your demeanor reassuring and loving, your chances are better than if you act otherwise.

Most people are frightened by the prospect of being questioned about their driving. Imagine how it would be for you, if you drive. One thing to avoid is telling the elder how it is going to be without discussing it. Being bossy, forceful, demanding, or accusatory can be very destructive and should be avoided.

It is no one's fault that we age. It is a fact of life that must be coped with, and your elder needs to cope. Allow for that to be. Anticipate that it may be upsetting to focus on the topic. Take your time. Be patient if you hear resistance. If it really is time to take the keys away, and the doctor is in agreement, be sure to mention that. Many elders look up to and go along with the doctor's word, even more than the family's word. It may even be best to arrange for the doctor to tell his patient that driving is no longer safe. If that cannot be done, you may have to tell her yourself.

The majority of elderly people will voluntarily give up the keys if asked to do so. However, there are still plenty of aging people out on the road who should not be driving.

WHAT CAN I DO WITH AN ELDER WHO HAS DEMENTIA AND STILL WANTS TO DRIVE?

A diagnosis of dementia in itself does not mean that you know whether someone is capable of driving or not. At the beginning of the disease process of Alzheimer's, for example, driving may still be safe, and the person may seem pretty normal. It is in the middle stage of Alzheimer's disease that driving becomes particularly problematic.

Though the middle stage may extend for three to five years, it is difficult to determine how far into the middle stage an elder has progressed. Therefore, it may be very difficult to predict when driving will become dangerous. It is imperative for anyone who has a loved one with a diagnosis of Alzheimer's disease or other dementia to closely watch your aging loved one for the first signs of unsafe driving.

You cannot leave it up to the elder to tell you when driving is becoming difficult. He may not have the perceptual ability to know this, since dementia is a progressive disease that damages the ability to remember as clearly as one could before having the disease.

With that understanding, you have to be on the alert that by the time your aging loved one has had early Alzheimer's or early dementia for two years, it is definitely time to look very carefully at the risks of allowing her to continue driving. Very close monitoring by you is going to be necessary for safety. If you are in doubt, it is clearly safer to take the car keys away or, if possible, to get the elder's agreement to give them up.

There is a fuzzy line between early dementia or early Alzheimer's and the middle stage, which creates problems for the family members and concerned caregivers. No one can be sure how long the transition from one stage to another takes, but we know from research that driving is definitely going to get dangerous at some point in the middle stage.

Therefore, the family member or concerned caregiver must be proactive and look for the trouble you know is coming. It is the only way to protect your elder unless he volunteers to give up driving of his own will. *Above all, we caution against waiting until there is an accident.* It is not fair to other drivers and pedestrians to ignore the possible safety risks from an elder's dangerous dementia.

There is no doubt that people are living longer and

that the risk of all dementias rises with age. The National Institute of Health estimates that one in seven people age seventy-one and older suffers from dementia. Alzheimer's is the most prevalent kind of dementia, and those eighty and older are much more likely to have dementia than those who are seventy. Additionally, those in this age group have a sharp increase in accidents. If your elder is eighty or older, do not expect him to be an exception. The risk is there.

WHAT CAN I DO TO MAKE IT EASIER FOR MY LOVED ONE TO GIVE UP DRIVING?

Although giving up driving is not easy, you can help. Start by communicating your respect for the difficulty that the loss of driving ability will mean to your elder. Acknowledge that the feeling of loss of control of one's driving must be really awful for the person going through it. Imagine having a brain disease that you know is going to get worse. Imagine how, little by little, you are aware of forgetting things and losing track of your daily activities. Imagine how hard it would be for an independent person to have to depend on others for basic things. Try to be as empathetic as possible, and invite your elder to talk about it if he wishes to do so. Listen with an open heart and a kind attitude.

An important part of having your aging loved one give up driving rights is making some concrete arrangements to transport him or her to necessary activities. If Mom likes to get her hair done and can't drive there anymore, provide a way for her to get to her hairdresser. Do not deprive Dad of his card game or other activities he loves when he can no longer drive.

Alternative Transportation

Alternative transportation in general can be hard to find. In some communities, it is expensive. Research transportation services for elders in your loved one's community. Some communities offer low-cost vans that pick up seniors at their residences and take them to appointments. Senior centers (sometimes called community centers) or other social service organizations in your parents' area may help solve the problem of transportation. Those who have the means may hire a home care worker to drive the elder to activities and appointments. Churches, synagogues, and other nonprofit organizations serving those in need may also have transportation services.

Public transportation can be an option if it is available near your elder's home, and if she can use it safely. However, if an elder is losing track of where she is, using the bus may not be safe, since a person with dementia can easily get lost. It may be up to family to provide the necessary transportation. If you live in a rural area where public transportation is not available, then family, friends, and local organizations must fill the need.

The Independent Transportation Network is an example of an organization formed to create community-based transportation services for seniors throughout the country. It was founded by Katherine Freund, whose then three-year-old son was struck and injured by a disoriented eighty-four-year-old driver who thought he had hit a dog. If your aging loved one is no longer able to drive and needs transportation, research available resources in your community.

A Change in Living Situation?

The absence of available transportation resources can force a change in living situation of an elder. Isolated seniors who may have to stop driving and who do not have transportation resources available near their homes may also find it difficult to get the necessities of life, such as groceries and doctor's appointments. This scenario may bring the elder's living situation to a crisis point. If your elder is in a location where no transportation is offered and you live far away, think this through before you bring up the subject of driving.

Sometimes the elder needs a little help with daily activities anyway and would consider an assisted living situation or a household helper. Most assisted living facilities provide transportation for their residents to doctors and to other social activities. If your aging loved one is at all ready to move to a supervised living setting, the issue of driving may be much easier to manage. A move could be the time to bring up giving up driving along with allowing the facility to provide transportation. For low-income seniors who have no community transportation options, family and friends may be the only alternatives.

As an example, James was living alone in his apartment for many years, and was completely independent before he suffered a massive stroke. He had been driving before the stroke. The damage he had from the stroke forced him to give up the car. He lives in assisted living now and relies on their van to take him to his appointments. It is actually very convenient. He can go anywhere in the city limits simply by asking for a ride on any of the three days a week it is offered. On other days or if he needs to go farther, he can make an appointment a day in advance. The cost is one dollar each way, which is very reasonable for him and fits his budget.

What Can I Do If My Elder Absolutely Refuses to Give Up the Car Keys?

Though a majority of aging people will voluntarily stop or give up driving when asked to do so, it is not unusual for an elderly driver to refuse to give up the car keys. This happens even if the family believes it is the right thing to do and tries to talk to the elder. Refusal is likely connected to the fear of losing control. As we age, we gradually lose control of some things we were always able to do before. Loss of control is a fear-provoking thing, and many people will fight to keep what they perceive of as control. They are losing a precious part of independence if they cannot drive any longer.

So, what can you do with this?

We advocate a five-level approach, with taking legal action as an absolute last resort when every other non-legal means has failed.

Five-Level Approach

Level 1: One-on-One Meeting

One can approach the subject of problematic driving in a tactful way, alone, at a quiet time, and when the elder seems to be in a good frame of mind. If tactful communication is not your strong suit, delegate to someone else who has this skill. Another family member, friend, or clergy may be willing to talk about this with your elder, one-on-one. Start with someone familiar who can remain calm. If you have siblings, choose the one most capable of having a difficult conversation or the person who feels closest to the elder.

If you are an only child or the only best friend of an

aging loved one, it is up to you. Be straight with your loved one. Tell your mom, "I'm concerned about your safety." Ask to talk about her ability to drive. If your elder has a trusted lawyer, especially one who has prepared the trust or will, it may be useful to contact the lawyer. Let the lawyer know of your concerns and ask for a meeting between your loved one and the lawyer.

However, remember that the attorney always represents his client, and that is not you. The lawyer can share your legitimate concerns about the elder's driving and may be a good source for the one-on-one meeting with your elder, especially if your loved one resists your advice. If this approach is not feasible or you are getting nowhere after several tries, consider moving to Level Two.

Level 2: Two-on-One Meeting

If using a one-on-one approach with you or a trusted other does not work, and your aging loved one refuses to discuss his driving, it is time to go to the next level. Using two family members or friends, or a combination, to bring up the subject together may yield the much-needed results.

Any combination of adult child and lawyer, family member and clergy, or other duo may be successful. This can be tricky, since the aging person may feel ganged up on if the twosome is forceful and pushy or if they fail to be respectful of the elder's resistance. It is always best to use the most liked, most favored, or most trusted persons available for this task. The elder may be willing to listen to two others whom he likes, respects, and gets along with to break the news that his driving has become a safety concern. If the two who approach the elder are both kindly in their approach, they have a better chance of success. Try more than once, if necessary. If that is also unsuccessful, it is time to try Level Three.

Level 3: Discussion with Professional Help

There are some people in the world who are just plain difficult, and if your elder is one of them, you may benefit from professional help with the issue of driving. Trained and skilled professionals, such as mediators, can do much to assist families get past this conflict-filled kind of conversation. It takes training to manage conflict among individuals who take opposing positions and then get stuck.

Mediation of a family conflict about driving is not just initiating or directing a conversation. Mediators are trained and skilled in getting to the root of conflict and particularly in bringing out the underlying emotions that often drive conflict.

We recommend use of a mediator or other trained, neutral person in situations where other attempts to work things out around a dangerous driver have failed. Bringing in a professional can make a great difference, particularly in that it will permit the aging person a forum in which to be heard and respected. Often, after all involved have had a chance to speak about their perceptions of the problem in front of a neutral person, it is far easier to come to an agreement about what to do.

Level 4: Intervention

If other approaches, including mediation, have failed, consider the idea of a family intervention. Intervention can mean many things, but in this context it refers to a number of persons approaching an individual who has a problem. It is sometimes used with individuals who have a problem with drugs or alcohol and are in denial about the problem.

As we suggest here, intervention is a technique in which a group of loved ones, including family, friends, and a leader (sometimes a professional such as an attorney, social worker, counselor, clergyperson, or health care professional) meets with the elder to discuss the subject of driving and the need to end the danger.

An intervention may raise concern with families or friends who are asked to participate. Some may feel that it is rude or intrusive, but an intervention to address a dangerous driver's risk can be a lifesaving event. It is a profound act of caring. An intervention requires an experienced person to lead the team and confront the driving issue with the reluctant or resisting elder.

While mediation aims to resolve conflict, the purpose of an intervention is to stop the danger presented by an elder's driving, reducing risk of injury or death to himself or to the public. It also differs from the kind of intervention used with those abusing a substance such as alcohol. Treatment is not the goal. The elder's problems of aging which cause him or her to be dangerous behind the wheel may not be amenable to treatment. Rather, the goal is to end the driving altogether.

The social worker or leader of the intervention is not neutral. Her role is to help the chosen team of family and friends approach the elder about unsafe driving in a way that is non-destructive. An intervention can be overwhelming to anyone who easily feels threatened, and the technique should be used very carefully, again with respect for the elder's point of view. The process must include an opportunity for the senior to speak about his point of view on the subject without interruption.

Then others in a position to observe the elder's driving ability can bring up their various points of view and suggestions. Remaining factual ("There was a near collision last week when you were driving," or "Your eye doctor says it isn't safe to drive now.") will be much more useful than being judgmental or saying anything the elder might think is insulting or demeaning ("You're a bad driver," or "Are you trying to kill someone?").

The goal of this kind of intervention is to persuade the aging person to give up the car keys voluntarily. The use of a team of loved ones, trusted professionals, and respected others, who are all in agreement that it must be done, can help the elder to make the decision with a measure of dignity. A statement such as, "All of us are worried about your driving since that ticket," or other consensus in the group can encourage a successful outcome. Reassurance to the elder that other means of transportation will be provided is essential. And remaining positive and loving throughout may lessen the blow to the elder, who may not have been aware of the concerns of family members and friends.

Everyone who participates in an intervention should be in agreement that the elder needs to give up driving. Do not invite anyone who may have a conflicted opinion, or who might believe the elder's driving ability is fine. This applies especially to any family or friends who are not in a position to know, who have not been driving with the elder.

A united front is a critical part of this technique. All persons who participate should speak in turn to the elder about their fears and concerns regarding the elder's driving and must say directly that they believe the elder must stop driving for his own safety, as well as the safety of others. The leader of the intervention can ask the elder to hand over the car keys. It is a form of peer pressure, in that everyone is in agreement that the elder is in danger if he continues to drive. It is a direct request to give up driving. It is an agreement to get the keys away, keeping the elder fully informed of why, even though he may be in complete denial.

The risks of using group intervention to approach the elder are that the elder may become very frightened, embarrassed, or resistant out of fear. He could lash out and become enraged. He could refuse to speak to anyone.

He could walk away and leave everyone sitting there. However, the risks may be worth the effort if you succeed. Having someone agree to give up driving rights is certainly better than forcing the decision on him. Preserving the elder's dignity is paramount. Stopping the dangerous behavior must occur if the intervention is to be successful.

Preparation for an intervention is critical. The leader must communicate with everyone and form a plan. The elder should be informed that this planning is taking place. Transparency of the planning process can reduce the suspiciousness and anger on the part of the elder.

We do not advocate hiding or stealing the car keys, using tricks, disabling the car without telling the elder, or other secretive methods to stop an elder from driving. All of these actions are dishonest and are more likely to cause the elder to become suspicious, enraged, or even punitive in retaliation for being tricked. It is only fair to discuss the possible plans with your elder, rather than have him go to get in the car and discover that it will not start because someone has disabled it.

One of our elderly clients whose family tried the above sneaky methods to get the elder to stop driving got so angry that he had another set of keys made and threatened to disinherit his daughter and son for taking his keys. They did not stop him from driving. Damage to the family relationships from the dishonesty of stealing the keys was devastating. Other approaches could have been tried, but they were not attempted. Eventually, it was the department of motor vehicles that did not renew his license and stopped the dangerous situation.

In another instance, an elder had had several minor fender bender accidents. Finally, she had a more serious collision and totaled her car turning in front of another driver. Fortunately, no one was injured. After the last accident, the family approached her to explain why they were not going to replace the car, a task she could not have done without their help.

It would have been much safer for this family to try one of the four steps recommended above before the final accident happened. They waited, because she kept saying, "I'm fine to drive." None of the adult children wanted to get in a fight with their mother about stopping her from driving. After the first or second minor accident, it was time to ask her to voluntarily give up her car keys. It was sheer luck that when she totaled the car, she did not hurt or kill anyone else. Do not let this be your elder. The gamble with safety is too great.

Level 5: Using the Law as a Last Resort

Finally, there are possible legal means that can be used as a last resort, but only if your aging loved one is truly a danger on the road in a specific and provable way. First, you could try the approach of requesting a letter from your elder's medical doctor to be sent to the local department of motor vehicles describing that the elder is no longer able to drive safely. Or you could ask your aging loved one's doctor to recommend an occupational therapist's evaluation of the elder's driving skills. That evaluation can add credibility to the report from an MD and give the MD greater security in the correctness of making a recommendation that the elder cease driving. Each state has a slightly different process, so ask at your local Department of Motor Vehicles to find out the process in your state.

State laws are not universal when it comes to aging drivers, so the result of communicating with the motor vehicle licensing department may vary from state to state. The local department of motor vehicles can issue a letter to a licensed driver, asking her to turn in the license voluntarily.

In California, a well-thought-out method exists. A similar method may be available in your parent's state. Anyone can anonymously request retesting of a driver who is impaired or believed to be unsafe to drive. A form is available on the Department of Motor Vehicles website (Request for Driver Reexamination), and it can be mailed in. The Department then contacts the driver and requests that she come in for a behind-the-wheel retesting for maintaining her license. If she fails, the license is revoked.

Typically, the state does not have the authority to suspend or revoke a driver's license unless the driver has failed a written, vision, or driving test at license renewal time. Another exception is if there has been an accident, traffic violation, or event that generates a police report, highway patrol report, or event that brings the aging driver before the court. In those instances, the traffic officer may recommend that the license of the offending driver be taken away. The court can decide to suspend or revoke a license. However, it will not necessarily do so based on the request of someone other than law enforcement.

A physician's letter to the state licensing department for motor vehicles can help. The licensing agency, in most states, has the authority to revoke a license based on a medical doctor's recommendation. This occurs with individuals who have seizure disorders, such as epilepsy, which can make a driver unsafe. The same concept can apply to an impaired older driver. With the results of the assessment showing that the elder is not a safe driver, the doctor is obligated to cooperate with efforts to end the elder's driving privileges. A letter to the department of motor vehicles from the physician, with the occupational therapist's driving assessment attached, may be enough to get the elder's license revoked.

DOES IT TAKE AN ACCIDENT TO STOP AN IMPAIRED DRIVER?

Sometimes it literally takes an accident for a police officer to see the elder, talk with her, and find evidence of confusion or disorientation to the degree that the officer believes the person who caused the accident should not be driving. Driving is a right, considered part of our freedom under the Constitution. Therefore, states are obligated to see proof that this right should be taken away in the interest of public safety. Even if there is an accident or incident, and the department of motor vehicles suspends or revokes a driver's license, the driver normally has a right to appeal this decision and request a hearing. In states where it works this way, the driver has the right to present evidence of her ability to drive, which could result in the suspension being lifted or changed.

Some elders even hire attorneys to represent them at such hearings and are successful in getting their driver's licenses restored. For others, however, the revocation of a license can become permanent. A hearing officer makes this decision based on evidence presented by both the driver and the motor vehicle department records.

Jackson's Case

Jackson was a well-respected business owner and long-time pillar of his community. Gradually, he began to develop cognitive impairment, but he continued to try to run his business and to drive. Either the damage to his brain from dementia actually prevented him from knowing he was impaired, or he did not wish to face that reality. He began to have numerous minor accidents in his highly visible, fancy car.

His auto insurance refused to allow any coverage but the most minor, even though he could well afford better insurance. He kept getting it fixed, and he kept driving.

His wife got worried. She knew that if he had a serious accident and there was very little insurance, anyone could sue them for their other assets. They were wealthy, and she did not want to take the ongoing risk. She sought advice.

The first recommendation I had was that she contact her husband's MD and ask him to request that Jackson be re-tested. Shortly after that, a request for retesting came in the mail. Jackson didn't tell his wife, but she knew. On the appointment day, Jackson went with a friend to the motor vehicle center and was retested. His wife noticed that he came home with his friend driving him. He said nothing to her about the results.

The next day, Jackson got up at his usual hour and drove to work. His wife searched his clothing from the day before. In his pants pocket, she found the driving test results. He had flunked. He had been required to surrender his license then and there, but he drove the next day anyway.

She and I discussed a strategy. She was to contact the police in their small town and bring in the driver's license test results. The police would then watch for him the next day and stop him on his way to work. His car was unmistakable.

Sure enough, the next day, Jackson got up as usual and drove to work. On his way, he was pulled over by the police officer, according to plan. Of course, when asked for his driver's license, he didn't have it, and the officer then searched the DMV record and found that his license had been revoked. He was driven home, and his car was impounded. His wife later sold it.

She arranged for a driver for him, something he had previously refused. He got used to the change rather well and at least that problem was solved.

This is one example of using the elder's doctor and law enforcement to get the job done. It worked in a small town where the car was known, but might be more difficult in a larger setting.

OTHER CONSIDERATIONS WHEN THE ELDER IS A DANGER TO HERSELF OR OTHERS

Suppose your elder is a dangerous driver, has nearly hit several cars, scares the life out of you when you are in the car with her, and you know she should not be driving. She refuses a driving assessment by an occupational therapist or anyone else, and her driver's license is good for two more years. You have tried to arrange a meeting, but she won't discuss it, and the two-person approach also failed. You don't know her doctor's name because she won't tell you.

Everyone in the family, and several neighbors and friends, tried the intervention approach, but she started screaming at everyone to get out of her house when the subject of driving came up. You are truly afraid—as is everyone in the family—that she is going to kill someone, maybe herself. She got lost in the grocery store last week and has fallen several times. She left the stove burner on last month without remembering and almost started a fire. She is unable to carry on a conversation and keep track of it. However, she still refuses to agree to limited driving and won't turn over the car keys. Is there anything else you can do?

There is one last thing to do, and it is the drastic step of guardianship—also called conservatorship in California. This is not meant to be a complete explanation of how it works. It is to mention it as a last resort, because some aging loved ones are too impaired to realize that they are unsafe, and someone must be appointed to make decisions for them. Briefly, getting a guardianship means going to court to get an order from a judge appointing someone to be a guardian, or conservator, of the person. That guardian then has authority to act for the person under guardianship. That authority includes legally stopping the elder from driving. In our hypothetical example above, the aging person does many dangerous things, and the issue is safety, to an extreme degree.

The lawyer preparing the matter for court can help you decide whether handling money is also an issue or not. It can be included in the guardianship proceeding as necessary. Aging persons who have trouble remembering to turn off the stove, get lost, and can't keep track of the conversation usually have problems handling money as well. The troubles they are having could be symptoms of dementia or other disease processes. These same disease processes can cause the driver to become unsafe behind the wheel.

The guardianship proceeding is not a simple matter. A lawyer is normally needed to help prove that an elder needs this serious protection, since a guardianship takes away major freedoms for the person upon whom it is imposed. The courts, through judges or commissioners who hear the evidence, are required to take steps to see that the rights of the individual are not taken away without very clear and weighty proof.

In other words, the evidence presented to the judge or commissioner that the elder should have a guardian must be very strong. The elder for whom guardianship is proposed has a right to present evidence that a guardianship is not needed. Therefore, in order to prove that many basic freedoms, which can include driving, should be taken away, the person asking for the guardianship for an elder has to have a doctor verify that the person is in serious danger without the guardianship.

In the earlier example of the elder with dementia (the elder who will not talk about her driving, has had near accidents, gets lost, keeps falling, leaves the stove on, etc.), testimony from witnesses would be needed to prove that these things occurred and that she is considered to be a danger to herself and others.

If there is sufficient proof, the judge may decide to grant the guardianship and will appoint a person, preferably a family member, to be the guardian of the elder in question. The guardian then has the legal right to take necessary precautions, including taking the car and keys away from the elder to protect the elder and others from danger.

Getting a guardianship is best done by an attorney experienced in these matters. Elder law attorneys are the most likely to have the necessary experience to handle this kind of case. We urge anyone who is thinking about a guardianship to seek legal advice and to consider the pros and cons very carefully before moving forward.

The risks of getting a guardianship are many. It costs money to hire an attorney to go to court. Even if the person seeking a guardianship has low income and qualifies for free legal services, there is a significant cost in terms of time and stress associated with the proceedings. It is possible that the elder could convince the court that her driving and other problems are not dangerous and that a guardianship is not needed. Skilled use of evidence is how lawyers win cases, including guardianship cases.

However, the decision is up to the judge. The courts are required to protect the rights of elders and must look very carefully at the reasons for the request for a guardianship. Therefore, guardianship is not automatically granted by the courts. In the earlier example of the difficult elder, she may hire an attorney of her own in an attempt to prevent the guardianship or conservatorship from being imposed. If the elder makes a good impression on the judge, speaks clearly, and appears to be of sound mind, the court may be unwilling to impose a guardianship. This can leave all parties involved angry, dissatisfied, and distrustful of each other.

An additional risk of a guardianship proceeding is that the elder may become very angry that she is being betrayed by the person(s) seeking to place her under a guardianship. It can fracture family relationships, cause emotional trauma to all involved, and leave a bitter, hostile family environment in its wake. However, this does not always happen. Sometimes the elder needs to have a judge appoint a guardian so that she can finally give up the car keys, as well as the other things that make her a danger to herself. It can resolve the matter and provide a means to protect the elder in many other ways as well. We call it a last resort, since it should only be used in extreme situations, when there is no alternative.

However, in the example described earlier, it is a reasonable choice of action. A car can certainly be a lethal weapon. A guardianship provides a legal way to stop a dangerous driver from injuring or killing anyone with a car. That being said, guardianship should never be attempted unless it is absolutely necessary for safety of the elder and safety of others.

Another important consideration about a guardianship or conservatorship is the fact that the guardian or conservator may not be honest or may not have the elder's best interests at heart. The risk increases when there is no family member willing to take on the burdensome responsibility of being the guardian, and the court appoints a stranger to the elder.

Guardians have almost unlimited power over the person who becomes their "ward" or protected person. As with any situation in which there is almost unlimited power, the temptation for unlimited corruption exists. Therefore, weigh the possibilities carefully, and use this legal means to protect the elder only when there is no reasonable alternative to preventing the most serious kinds of harm.

The Parker Case

Here is a true story of a dangerous older driver. One wonders why the family, friends, clergy, or doctor of ninety-three-year-old Ralph Parker of St. Petersburg, Florida, did not seek a guardianship over him prior to this incident in 2005. He struck and killed a pedestrian, and then drove three miles with the dead (victim's) body lodged in his windshield.

According to The American Bar Association publication, *Experience*, which reported this story in its Winter 2008 issue[1], Mr. Parker thought the body "had fallen from the sky." Surely someone must have known before this tragedy that Mr. Parker was a danger to himself and others. He should not have been driving, yet he was. Perhaps he thought he was fine. Do not let this happen your elder.

Common Danger Signs that the Older Driver Should Stop Driving

The best way to determine, on your own, if your aging loved one should stop driving is to get in the car and see for yourself how they are doing behind the wheel.

From the Texas Aging Network's Senior Driving Assessment Checklist, consider these actions:

- Did your driver stop for red lights or misinterpret signs and signals?

- Did your driver appear to notice other vehicles, pedestrians, bicycles, or road hazards?

- Did he have a near miss?

- Did he not look over his shoulder when pulling away from the curb?

- Did he yield when necessary pulling out of a driveway?

- Did he drift into other lanes, not use the turning lane, or not maintain a safe distance from the car in front?

- Did he drive too slowly, too aggressively, or too fast?

- Did he get confused or irritated with other drivers?

- Did he fail to anticipate potential danger or changing traffic conditions, such as slowing down when brake lights appeared ahead?

SUMMARY

Driving is a right in our society for those who can pass the driving tests and get a license. Giving up this right or having it taken away is a serious matter. Loss of control is very important to most of us. It is unfair to others to ignore a dangerous older driver, despite the reality that the elder may lose the right to drive. Caring family members must collect information, approach the subject respectfully, and, in some cases, take steps to limit or end the dangerous driver's chances of injuring himself or someone else.

If you are looking for additional resources about elders and driving, including ways to safely extend driving and other information, I suggest additional resources in Appendix A.

Recommended Resources

- Rosenblatt, Carolyn. "A Car Is a Lethal Weapon." www.Forbes.com/sites/carolynrosenblatt/2012/08/15/dangerous-older-drivers-a-car-is-a-lethal-weapon. Forbes. Accessed January 17, 2015.

- Bertschler, Patricia, and Laurette Cocklin. *Truce! Using Elder Mediation to Resolve Conflict among Families, Seniors, and Organizations.* Ohio: NCS Publishing, 2004.

- P. Callone, C. Kudlacek, and B. Basiloff, *A Caregiver's Guide to Alzheimer's Disease.* New York: Demos Medical Publishing, 2003.

- Johnson, Vernon E. *Intervention: How to Help Someone Who Doesn't Want Help.* Minneapolis, MN: Johnson Institute Books, 1986.

- Texas Aging Network. PO Box 700291, Dallas, TX 75370. www.TexasAgingNetwork.com.

FIVE THINGS YOU NEED TO KNOW ABOUT CARING FOR AGING PARENTS

FROM A DISTANCE

Many of us do not live close to our aging parents. We are scattered across states and countries. And when their health begins to fail, we start to worry. Who would care for them if they lose independence? How can I help when I'm so far away? Helping from a distance can be difficult. Keeping track of aging parents when you do not see them often is a challenge. In hundreds of conversations with adult children and plenty of research on this subject, I have collected a few pointers to help the adult children who live far from their loved ones. A main consideration is safety, and we address that in this chapter. Another consideration is whether there should be a physical move. A third concerns avenues of help that you can find if you have to remain at a distance.

My husband, Mikol, and I are what is called "distance caregivers." As I've mentioned before, my husband's mother, Alice, is ninety-two years old, lives independently, and still drives. She is hundreds of miles away. So far, so good, but this will not last forever in all likelihood. I will share with you our personal experiences and what we have done to cover our bases in the event of an emergency or mishap. Here are the five points we go into in this chapter. These are things every distant adult child needs to know to be prepared for caregiving.

Five Preparation Points for Adult Children

1. Plan for your parent's possible need for help.

2. Keep contact information for your parents' friends and neighbors with you.

3. Consider hiring a care manager to help you.

4. Insist on having conversations about your parents' ability to pay for care.

5. Talk about end-of-life wishes so you can honor them.

A False Sense of Security?

I often hear clients who have loved ones in another state, or even another country, tell me their eighty-plus-year-old parent is doing fine, and thank goodness she is so independent. I am as happy for them as I am for my husband and myself that, at this moment, we don't have responsibility for parent-care day in and day out. But realistically, we do not expect Alice to be perfectly okay until the end of her life. We are in the aging consulting business, and we know of a lot of things that can suddenly or gradually destroy an elder's independence. We are prepared with numerous alternatives for Alice, and we hope you will be prepared in your family, too.

Having an independent parent is a gift, but it is prudent to think of it as a gift that can change in a moment, and without warning. No matter what your loved one's state of physical and mental health is right now, you must consider the probability that nearly all of us will need help at some point as we age, especially as we live past eighty-five, which the federal government terms: "the oldest old." That brings me to the first thing you need to remember:

PLAN FOR YOUR PARENT'S POSSIBLE NEED FOR HELP

Your aging parent will probably need your help at some point down the road, and you need to talk about it and plan for it.

Many people do not want to face the possibility of infirmity and will do anything to avoid the subject. You, yourself, may be uncomfortable with the idea that your parent could become dependent on anyone else, especially *you*, and you, too, may avoid the subject. The reluctance you feel is natural, but it must be overcome unless you like the feeling of panic and extreme stress better than the idea of getting past discomfort.

Panic and extreme stress are the consequences of an aging parent emergency or trauma—if you are unprepared.

Alice's Emergency

Alice lives about 600 miles away from us. One can't jump on a plane any hour and get there. Flights are less frequent than they would be to a big city. The only other family member is my husband's sister, who is two hours' drive away—and that's in good traffic. California is not known for good traffic conditions.

One afternoon, my husband's cell phone rang. He saw that it was Alice calling, and he said, "Hi, Mom." A deep male voice said, "I'm Officer Smith, and I'm with Alice here. She seems to have fainted, and we are taking her to the hospital." He said she was okay and responding to questions, but seemed woozy. He told us where they were. He gave the phone to her, and a few words were exchanged just before the ambulance came.

You can't help but feel a terrible sense of urgency in this situation. What was wrong? Why had she fainted?

She had high blood pressure, and we always worry about a stroke. Did she have one? What should we do?

We were partially prepared for this, but not completely. We at least had taken one step that every distance caregiver needs to take, which was to have the names and phone numbers of two of her friends in our cell phone contacts folder. Mikol called Alice's best friends. They agreed to go over to the hospital as quickly as possible to see her and to let us know what was happening.

We also had the name of a neighbor in our cell phones. Mikol called the neighbor, who kindly went to the emergency room right away and called us to tell us Alice was being seen by a doctor. Eventually, the doctors figured out that she had passed out due to a recent adjustment in her blood pressure medication and that she was okay. She was able to return home that night.

Her friends brought Alice home and checked in on her early in the morning. Being the independent type, she wouldn't stay at their house that night, insisting that she was fine.

The episode caused us to have many conversations about how to deal with any falls or episodes where Alice might need help immediately. She had an alert pendant (which some call a personal emergency response system), but, of course, refused to wear it. The pendant has a button on it that allows her to call someone if she falls and is conscious enough to push it. Hers has a GPS tracker on it too, so it can be used outside her home, in the car, etc.

She reluctantly agreed to make better use of it after that emergency.

That brings me to the second thing to remember:

KEEP CONTACT INFORMATION FOR YOUR PARENTS' FRIENDS AND NEIGHBORS WITH YOU

Have your aging parents' immediate contacts, friends, and neighbors in your cell phone or mobile device so you can reach them at a moment's notice.

It could be a call you receive in the middle of the night from a paramedic or from an emergency room. You might be so shocked by a call you receive that you can't remember where or whom to call. Keep the information in the most likely form for you to be able to find it, even if you are not thinking clearly. "Mom's Friends" might be the name for a folder where all the necessary information is kept.

You also need to discuss this with your aging parent. Who are the best friends? The most willing neighbors? The closest people able to assist? One thing to keep in mind is that if your parent is among "the oldest old," his friends might be in the same age group and not able to step in, drive, or be of help to you.

Alternatives

Alice has been widowed for a few years now. She does not want to move closer to either of her adult children, since her friends, her familiar community, and her enjoyment of life is where she is now. What could we do if we needed "boots on the ground" in a hurry or for rehabilitation after an event?

Again drawing on our considerable experience in the field of aging and elder care, I suggested that we get a professional care manager to be in the wings, so to speak, should we ever need someone to help us with Alice in an emergency.

Most people have never heard of a professional geriatric care manager (PGCM). The field is not one which is licensed, so the title can mean just about anything. There are some ideal standards of what a care manager is supposed to do, but there is no licensing body to ensure that those standards will be met. Because our aging population is increasing rapidly and people are living longer than ever, the need for professional help with our aging parents has created a newer kind of worker. The geriatric care manager is usually a nurse or licensed social worker. However, there are many geriatric care managers who are neither one of those and who have no license in any field. They may or may not have training in gerontology (the study of aging). Some have had a lot of experience in the community caring for their own aging parent, and they set themselves up in the field, since they have learned all the local resources and can be of help in connecting clients to these resources.

A care manager is a person who will interview your parent, assess her needs, and develop a care plan or management plan with you or your loved one. The best managers know a variety of workers and resources to meet the needs they identify in their assessment of your parent. They should know good geriatric doctors, senior centers, and programs appropriate for your parent's situation.

For example, if your father is getting frail and needs help with chores at home, the geriatric care manager could find and refer you to a competent and reliable home care agency, so your parent could get help at home. If various things are going on at once, the care manager can coordinate transportation, workers, medical visits, and other supports.

When a crisis hits, a nearby geriatric care manager can get to the parent faster than you can if you live at a distance. Further, the care manager can do a lot of preventive care for elders and can promote safety and good quality of life.

That brings us to the third thing to remember:

CONSIDER HIRING A CARE MANAGER TO HELP YOU

A care manager can be your eyes and ears nearby your parent.

How to Find and Use a Care Manager

You will not typically meet a care manager through your doctor or health clinic. You will not find their services covered under Medicare or most other health insurance plans. Payment is out of pocket, and rates vary from place to place and state to state. There is no standardization of their hourly fees. An easy way to find a care manager is through an Internet search, which is how we found one for Alice.

Because no license is required, care managers are not monitored by state departments of health or social services. Yet, this kind of service can make a world of difference in what happens to your aging loved one and how he is cared for. You need to be a good consumer and ask questions when you search for a manager for your parent.

Care managers, even if they are licensed nurses, do not provide direct care themselves. Rather, they are the ones who can see that care is provided. (A licensed nurse can only deliver care through a licensed agency that provides home health care.)

Some of the things a care manager can do for you include the following:

- **Make doctor and dentist appointments for your elder, and accompany your elder to the appointments.** They can talk to the health care provider about health problems that need attention, especially if your elder loved one is forgetful of the problems or has difficulty explaining them. They can report to you what happened and ask any questions you want asked of the health care provider. If your aging parent keeps telling you "everything's fine" after doctor's visits, when you know everything isn't fine, having someone qualified to accompany Mom or Dad to the doctor or dentist can be very useful. Care managers can also provide transportation to appointments for those who have no other alternatives and who do not drive.

- **Interview, screen, and monitor in-home helpers, such as companions, aides, and other workers.** Getting a little help at home can assure that your aging loved one remains in his home as long as possible. However, the difficulty of locating a safe, honest, in-home helper can be beyond the capability of some impaired or frail elders. The very reasons your elder may need help in the first place can interfere with his ability to get that help independently. For example, plenty of elders have impaired vision, hearing, and memory. Your mother may not use the Internet. Your father may not be able to recall whom he spoke to on the telephone yesterday. A competent care manager can solve the problem of hiring a helper and ongoing monitoring of the work the helper is doing.

- **Visit the elder—when you are unable to do so yourself—and report to you.** We finally hired the care manager against Alice's resistance just in case. If she had a fall but didn't need to go to the doctor, or if she got into any kind of trouble and we needed someone to check on her, we now have a competent person to do that.

- **Act as an advocate for your elder at the hospital, assisted living facility, or other location where your elder may not be able to speak well for herself.** Hospitals can be dangerous places, as can other long-term care facilities. The chronic, nationwide nursing shortage is no small contributor to the danger of being in a hospital. Unfortunately, about 100,000 people per year die in the United States as a result of preventable medical errors. If your elder loved one needs to go to a hospital, and you live far away, it is safest to have someone visit every day for as long as family members and friends are available. If they are not available, a geriatric care manager who is a nurse can do this task and report to the

family members for as long as the family desires
and can afford to have this specialized help at hand.

- **Maintain records your elder may need, such as
  medical, prescription, financial, or legal papers,
  and make them accessible to you when you need
  them.** If your aging loved one has trouble keeping track of paperwork such as bills, bank statements, or other documents, it can create a serious
  problem. In our practice, one client's mother had
  been paying her Medicare supplemental insurance
  until she fell and was hospitalized. The adult child
  nearby could not find any organized paperwork, so
  she did no bill paying. The supplemental insurance
  was cancelled for lack of payment of premiums.
  The hospitalization generated enormous charges,
  many of which were not covered by Medicare. We
  were able to advocate for the elder and get the
  supplemental insurance reinstated, but it was an
  expense for the family members and the elder to
  pay for professional legal services to straighten out
  the mess after the fact.

  It would have been far more efficient and less
  expensive to retain a geriatric care manager to organize all of the bills and monthly expenses before
  disaster struck. Then the adult children would have
  had the necessary information in one place when
  Mom had to go to the hospital, and the insurance

premiums would have gotten paid on time, averting the cancellation.

- **Help you with the decision to move your family member out of the family home when the time comes, and assist with all the details of moving. They can also help you choose the right place to go.** If your loved one is not able to manage safely at home any longer, she must go to another location which provides supervision. Locating the right place can be a very time-consuming chore. It should involve visiting prospects with and without your elder to see how they feel to you. Knowing the reputation of all the facilities in the area, reading the contracts, understanding what is involved in the move, and planning ahead for the many details of moving out of the family home can be very daunting. A geriatric care manager can take some or the whole load off your shoulders. As someone outside the family, the care manager can also offer advice to the elder, which may not be as suspect as advice from adult children in dealing with a parent who is resistant to change.

- **Provide information about social activities, safety, adult day health services, senior centers, equipment, transportation, meals, and other things your elder's community may offer to enrich and improve your elder's life.** If you live in the same neighborhood as your aging loved one, you may not need help with knowing how to find suitable activities for your elder. However, most children of elders have not involved themselves with activities for seniors and may not know the community resources or how to find them. Doing what you can to prevent social isolation can keep your elder safer, but may not be so easy if you don't know where to find services. A mere Internet search, without knowing about a specific organization or center, may not give you enough information. A care manager should know how to find enjoyable activities for your parent and can take her there to get acquainted if you are unable or not ready to do it yourself.

Answers to Common Questions About Care Managers

What Is the Availability of a Care Manager?

The PGCM is typically available to you twenty-four hours a day, seven days a week. In many ways, hiring this kind of assistant for your family is an investment in the safe keeping and quality of life of your elder loved one.

What Are Care Managers Not Allowed to Do?

A care manager cannot give legal or financial advice. Some care managers assist with budgeting and household money management, such as paying bills, and can even help with selling the family home. However, a care manager is generally not a money handler for the elder's estate and must avoid any impropriety concerning the elder's finances. If there is no local family member to handle an elder's finances, it is best to have a licensed professional, such as a fiduciary, do this.

If a care manager takes on the task of paying bills or other chores which permit access to the elder's bank account or other money, a family member should monitor all financial expenditures. Ideally, this is done online, so that another responsible person can see the activity in any account and can check for questionable activity or mistakes.

Is There Any Way to Pay for Care Management Other Than out of Pocket?

The national range of charges from a care manager may vary from a minimum of $80 dollars per hour to $200 dollars per hour. If your elder loved one has the resources and wants to stay in her own home, this option may help you to accomplish that for your loved one safely. Some kinds of long-term care insurance, especially newer products purchased since 2007, may provide for some kinds of professional care management in the home. Some policies of long-term-care insurance may even provide their own care managers.

Otherwise, care management is generally not covered by Medicare, Medicaid, or private health insurance. The cost is usually paid out of pocket.

How Do You Find a Qualified and Experienced Professional Geriatric Care Manager?

A search in your local community is one place to start. There is also an organization, The National Association of Professional Geriatric Care Managers (NAPGCM), and you can check the website for listings of geriatric care managers. This website enables you to compare and contrast professionals before you contact someone you might want to interview.

The National Association of Professional Geriatric Care Managers is located at:

1604 N. Country Club Road

Tucson, AZ 85716-3102

Telephone: (520) 881-8008

Website: CareManager.org

It is helpful to be cautious of any person you hire to help with caring for aging loved ones. Without licensing requirements, there is no criminal background check, fingerprinting, competency requirement, or testing to determine whether the person calling himself a geriatric care manager is actually qualified to do the job properly. Those who hold a license in another discipline, such as nursing or social work, are tested, screened, and checked by the state to establish at least minimum competency for that licensing.

If the person you are considering as a care manager has a license in nursing or social work, ask to see the license to be sure it is current. The state boards which regulate both nursing and social work may provide current licensing status online through the state in which the care manager is located. Finally, ask for references and check them out before you make the decision to hire.

Hiring a Care Manager for Alice

As a retired RN myself, I admit to a preference for licensed nurses as care managers. My reasons are that the person has been vetted and fingerprinted by the state licensing board, and the RN can ask sophisticated health questions, see the known side effects of many medications, and communicate with your loved one's MDs in a way most non-nurses can't. If they visit regularly, they can also spot signs of developing health problems that may require attention.

Since my husband and I do not know all the resources in Alice's area, we went to the care manager website. I looked for Alice's city, and searched for an RN. I found one and contacted her and asked her to see Alice, who is much more independent than most ninety-two-year-olds. She went and did her assessment, and we expected her to be available in the event of any problem, which was the point of having her. When a problem did come up, we called.

No response.

She was out of town. She did not have a backup. She had not notified us. This was very unprofessional.

Although we had gone through the expense of hiring her and paying a sum for her assessment of Alice, she clearly was not going to be there when we needed her—back to the website. We found another RN who gave the impression of being much more responsible. She visited Alice more than once and later updated her information with Alice by phone. We expect that if we need her, she will be there.

Alice, who is stubbornly independent, did not think she needed a care manager and was very reluctant to let us hire one. We paid for the expense to lessen that resistance. To us, after the panicky feelings we had at the time of her fainting episode, it is worth it. The care manager has had little to do, since Alice has not had any emergencies of late, but we feel safe in the knowledge that someone is there if Alice's needs or situation changes.

INSIST ON HAVING CONVERSATIONS ABOUT FINANCES

Resistance to talking about money creates a serious problem for the adult children of aging parents. As we have described, most of us are reluctant to face the real possibility that we could ever become dependent on others for care or that we will even lose any of our independence. Ignorance about a parent's finances and resistance to facing the probable need for care is a risky combination. You can get stuck with a sudden responsibility you don't want or are ill prepared to handle.

This brings us to the fourth thing every adult child must remember: start and insist on the conversations about parents' ability to pay for care.

Why is it necessary to discuss your parents' ability to pay for care? Because if you don't, you may end up in a very expensive mess should a sudden change happen in their lives and you are forced to take responsibility. If they need care and cannot pay for it, they may be eligible for various public benefits. These take time and planning to get, and you might need help on short notice. Planning ahead can make a huge difference in your loved one's ability to access any benefit for which they are eligible.

For instance, many people do not know about Veterans' benefits that can help pay for home care or care in assisted living. The information is available for free on the Internet. There are a lot of requirements to meet and many forms to fill out. The process takes months, even when a person is eligible. If you discuss it before the event of any emergency, you have a much better chance of figuring out when and where to apply for a benefit such as this.

The same applies to Medicaid, which is for low-income individuals. Eligibility varies from state to state, and there are numerous eligibility standards that must be met. Planning even years in advance can be a great advantage, if you can look ahead and speak with a lawyer about what your parents need to do to become eligible. But if you never consider that long-term care is a possibility and then find out your parents have little or nothing to pay for it, you could be in a very stressful situation when the unexpected happens.

These public benefits programs are discussed in more detail in the last chapter of this book. For those of you with low-income or limited-resource aging parents, that chapter is one you must read.

Steven's Story

Steven is forty-nine, and his father is sixty-nine and divorced. His father has a chronic illness that was initially controlled with medication. Dad was still working full-time and supporting himself. He lives in a different state from Steven. One afternoon, Steven's father called him to let him know that the medication stopped being effective, he is now ill, and he can't return to work.

Steven is an only child. He and his father had never had a single conversation about Dad's finances prior to this, despite the risk of the chronic illness and the risk of Dad at some point being unable to work. Dad can get Social Security, but that will not be enough to live on, much less pay for any kind of care, should he need it.

No advance planning for anything has been done. Steven is totally bewildered by all of this. He now understands that he is probably going to have to help his father, but he has no idea how that is going to work or if he can afford it.

Steven does not have a Durable Power of Attorney for Finances for his father. His father owns a house, but Steven has just learned that Dad has no savings, no retirement account, and no assets other than the house. He needs Medicaid, but did not apply for it. He is ill and will need help at home. How will Dad manage?

Steven has a great deal of work to do in a very short time. He is feeling terrible pressure, and he is angry with his father for leaving him in the position of not knowing anything in advance.

Could this have been prevented? Yes, if both Steven and his father had insisted on better communication and having the necessary conversations about Dad's finances. There were alternatives available, and things could have been done to protect Dad from being forced into the urgent situation in which he now finds himself.

Frances's Story

Frances has two parents, both in their late eighties living in the home where they've been for over fifty years. Their home is valuable, despite being neglected for a long time. They have assets in the bank, but Frances does not know what they are. They change the subject when anyone talks about money.

Frances's father, Theo, has been caring for her stubborn mother, Virginia, who is disabled and can't walk independently. Then Theo fell, and he went first to the hospital and then to assisted living. He can't manage the stairs, and he can't come home. Frances is forced to deal with her very difficult mother with both resistance to help and disabilities, and she is very frustrated, because she has no information about how to pay for the care her mother needs. She doesn't even know where to find the checkbook to pay the assisted living home for her father. Her mother has forgotten where it is.

This situation required professional help from me to get Frances the Durable Power of Attorney signed by both of her parents. I went to Virginia's home with Frances to persuade her to do this, since she had resisted even talking about it prior to that time. Theo was more cooperative, but Frances was running back and forth between both parents. She was overwhelmed trying to figure out the budget, how the bills got paid, how much was in the checking account, and where the other assets were located. She took a leave from her full-time job to do all of this. It was a mess that took months to straighten out.

Frances had always been reluctant to push her parents to discuss finances with her. She knew she needed to be better prepared in case something happened—which it did—but she didn't want to upset them. She needed to get past her own discomfort and insist on the necessary conversations about finances. Fortunately for her, Theo and Virginia had enough assets to pay for the care they both required. She was finally able to get her mother to go to the same assisted living facility where Theo was, and she fixed up and rented out their house to help support them.

Her aggravation, the need to take unpaid leave from her job, and the extreme stress could have been avoided if she had insisted and persisted in having the necessary conversations about finances.

If you chose only one thing to do after reading this part of the things to remember, let it be that you work with your aging parents to get a Durable Power of Attorney for finances.

TALK ABOUT END-OF-LIFE WISHES SO YOU CAN HONOR THEM

If money matters are somewhat of a touchy subject, end of life seems to be an absolutely taboo one for most

Americans. It has been said that we are the only country that considers death to be optional. Consider how we often refer to death—"in case anything ever happens to me"—as if it won't. Our culture has a phobia about the entire subject. Some people seem to think that if you don't ever discuss it, it won't happen.

Never talking about the natural end of the life cycle can lead to more heartache than you ever need to experience. If you are able to learn what your aging loved ones want as they near their last days or the last part of life, you will be much more prepared when the time comes.

This brings me to the fifth thing everyone needs to remember:

Talking about your aging parent's last wishes will make it possible for you to honor their wishes.

If you do not know what your loved ones want as they grow older and they get to the last part of their lives, you may be forced to make decisions for them without knowing for sure what they wanted. Worse yet, if you have no clear direction, the medical establishment will decide for you, and they will do a lot of things most people don't want done. The following story is an example from my own life.

Joe's Story

When my father-in-law, Joe, was in his eighties, I insisted that we have a discussion about his last wishes and Alice's (my mother-in-law) as well. Did he want to be kept alive by artificial means should he be unable to speak for himself? Would he want to be cared for at home if he had a lingering illness? We went into detail. I made sure both of my in-laws had an Advance Healthcare Directive, appointing someone to be their agent to ensure that their wishes were carried out. They appointed my husband, Mikol, rather than his more emotionally driven sister, to be his agent, as discussed in a prior chapter. That meant it would be his job to advocate for his father's wishes if it became necessary.

Some years later, Joe was diagnosed with pancreatic cancer with little warning that he was becoming ill. A failed surgery and three weeks later, it was clear that he was failing and was unlikely to leave the hospital. The hospital was a busy teaching facility with many interns and residents learning from each patient's case. When my father-in-law began to lose ground in one body system, they added more medication. When another failed, they added even more drugs to bolster his functioning.

After speaking frankly to the ICU nurses, it was clear to me that he was not going to survive and that all the frenzy of medication, interns, residents, and other physicians were only prolonging the inevitable. These were artificial means of keeping him alive, the exact thing he had said he did not want. At that time, he was unconscious, attached to a ventilator to keep him breathing, and had eight different IV lines in his arms—all but one of them for things other than pain relief. This was not right. They would have kept it up for perhaps weeks longer unless someone stopped them.

Mikol was struggling, of course. I had the opportunity to speak to him privately and quietly about Joe's Healthcare Directive. His emotional response was that he did not sign up to play God. I helped him see that God is playing God, and that all Mikol had to do was to speak up for his father's wishes and see that they were honored. That meant no drawn-out, futile efforts to keep him going when none of it was going to make him better. None of the physician's efforts would have stopped the inevitability of his passing. Still, Mikol needed to sleep on it.

The next morning, he called the ICU and spoke to the nurse. A string of more tests, invasive ones, had been scheduled. He reminded them that he was Joe's spokesperson, and he wanted all but the pain medication to stop. They complied, and the tests were cancelled. The slew of extra IVs was gradually stopped. Joe was able to reach the end of life in a peaceful and dignified way, without the unnecessary interference of useless drugs that seemed to only serve as teaching tools for the medical students.

If we had not had a discussion with Joe earlier in his life about his last wishes, and if we had not been able to advocate for what he wanted, he might have been kept alive artificially for quite some time before they were willing to give it all up. The lesson here is that you need to have the discussion. You need to find out what your aging parent wants. If you do not do so, the doctors and the hospital administration—people who never met your loved one—will be making all the important end-of-life decisions. That may not be what your aging parent wants. I know it's not what I want.

Free Tools to Help You with This Subject

A lot of people are highly uncomfortable talking about end-of-life issues—last wishes: Those things that your parent actually wants. Sometimes they are so uncomfortable that they avoid it and avoid it and avoid it until it's too late. Then, you have no guidance. You have to guess, and the doctors in charge might not agree with you. Your other family members might not agree with you, either.

Fortunately, some knowledgeable people have come up with helpful online tools. Best of all, they're free. The American Bar Association (ABA), the largest organization of lawyers in the United States, has done some amazing work for the public. The problem is that few people know about the work they've done. Few people have used the publications that very experienced attorneys have put together and posted after much thought. So, here's my effort to bring their work to you.

Here's what we know from research about getting a document done and signed: It doesn't assure you that what you asked for will be followed. My father-in-law's case was a good example. He checked off the boxes, signed the document, and did all he was supposed to do, but the physicians still ignored the paper, which was in Joe's chart at the hospital. We call the document an Advance Healthcare Directive, a power of attorney for healthcare, a healthcare proxy, a living will, and a few other things. No matter what you call it, every state recognizes that you have a right to spell out what you want at the end of your life, and you have the choice to put it in writing. So why don't people follow the directives?

There are a lot of reasons. Doctors are afraid of getting sued if they let you die without doing things to you to keep you going. They may be uncomfortable with watching a patient die without doing all that they can. The forms themselves need someone to back them up, and that might be *you* if you are appointed as agent on a healthcare directive. I want to encourage you to have open communication with your aging parent so that you are very clear about what she wants done and not done.

To help with communication and to get you and your aging parent to think this through, the ABA has created a Consumer's Toolkit for Health Care Advance Planning. You can find it at www.AmericanBar.org under "Resources."

You can also go to the ABA website and search for "Consumer's Toolkit for Health Care Advance Planning." It contains a set of ten tools that can each be downloaded separately.

I like the questions it asks, such as, "Are some

conditions worse than death?" and "How do you weigh odds of survival?"

I decided to see if my own adult children could answer the questions about what I would want near the end of life, should I be unable to speak for myself, as Joe was. In the toolkit, there is a Proxy Quiz for family and physician. It has a page of questions about what the family member thinks you would want. They take the quiz and then you see how accurate they were. I gave both my kids the quiz, separately. Both did very well, maybe because I've hammered them with this info for some time.

So, even if you feel uncomfortable with bringing up the end of life and last wishes, you can get some really good help from these tools. There are even conversation scripts and ideas for how to deal with your parents' resistance. I encourage you to use them. Each one is short—about a page or two—and it is in plain language, easy to use and understand. If you need an excuse to get started with the conversation, you can always blame it on me or your attorney.

SUMMARY

This discussion is directed at those whose parents do not live nearby, but it can really apply to anyone.

First, we need to expect that our aging loved ones may need help, and we, as adult children, must anticipate what to do when that time comes. Open and honest discussions may not be your aging parents' strong suit, so starting the conversation might be up to you.

Be ready for the call in the middle of the night or a sudden event when you are too far away to get there fast. Have those local contacts in your own phone or device. Consider finding a professional care manager to help you if you are like I am, with a ninety-two-year-old mother-in-law living 600 miles away. You need to be able to call someone who can get there fast and tell you what's going on.

All of the services you are probably going to need to make life easier for yourself and your loved one will cost money. The subject of finances has to be discussed, even if your parent resists. It's up to you to insist on having discussions about whether your parents can afford to pay for care and whether they can meet the eligibility requirements for public benefits, such as Medicaid.

Finally, there is nothing worse than anguish over what to do when your aging parent is near the end of life and decisions have to be made when you don't know what to do. Free tools from the ABA can help you. We hope that at least some part of this chapter will get the wheels moving and spur some action on your part. I hope this will help you be as prepared for your parent's changes in health as you can be.

Recommended Resources

- American Association of Retired Persons (AARP). 601 E Street NW, Washington, DC 20049. www.AARP.org.

- "American Bar Association Consumer's Toolkit for Health Care Advance Planning." www.AmericanBar.org/groups/ law_aging/resources/health_care_decision_making/ consumer_s_toolkit_for_health_care_advance_planning. html. Accessed Aug. 1, 2014.

- The National Association of Professional Geriatric Care Managers. 1604 N. Country Club Road, Tucson, AZ 85716-3102. www.CareManager.org.

WILL YOU NEED TO
HELP
YOUR AGING PARENTS
FINANCIALLY?

In my work consulting with and advising families about aging loved ones, the issue comes up quite often: will I have to support my parents if they run out of money?

Because people are living longer than ever before in our history, those who planned to make it financially on Social Security with perhaps a modest pension may find themselves unable to do so. This chapter explores two key points to help you and your aging parents be prepared.

Two Keys to Being Prepared Financially:

1. The vital need for advance planning, and how adult children can help their aging loved ones plan ahead responsibly

2. Understanding and making use of any available benefits

Most adult children whose parents are not wealthy harbor a secret or emerging fear that they are going to have to come up with money every month for their elders. It is a daunting thought, since so many people have struggled through the major recession in our country and have their own financial recovery to do. They're busy with families of their own, and, perhaps, they are planning and saving for their own retirement.

We applaud the major advances in medicine and technology because they have increased our longevity, but they don't come without consequences. Just as we are glad that our elders can survive the things that used to end lives much earlier, we also have more infirm elderly in our midst than ever before.

The consequences of long life have an inescapable impact on families. We hope to encourage family conversations with the information in this chapter. The "what if" scenarios need to be talked about, and not just once. The subject needs to be a series of talks about your elders' current financial status, the possible need for care, and how your elders are going to pay for what they need in the future.

Families also need to discuss in some detail how a low-income loved one without assets will manage if she is unable to work in the future. If adult children will one day need to step up and support an aging parent who lives a long time, the planning needs to start years ahead of time.

THE PROBLEM: "I NEVER THOUGHT I WOULD LIVE THIS LONG"

Many an octogenarian, or someone even older, has said this in my office while talking about finances with an adult child present. They come for information and guidance. The older person, perhaps in his late 80s or 90s has a little savings, but it is quickly being depleted because he has to pay for a helper at home. And almost invariably, the elder wants to remain in his own home. He usually has Social Security and a small pension of perhaps $400–$700 a month. Total income for these elders is a little too much for them to qualify for Medicaid, which would open the door to various benefits, but it is still not enough to pay for the care they need, not even enough for in-home care a few hours a week—everyone is worried.

This is not an unusual scenario. Most older people in our country are not wealthy. Many worked all their lives and earned a retirement income. Or, for many women who did not work outside the home, their spouses earned the pension, and they are beneficiaries under the pension plan. But a pension designed fifty years ago, or more, did not include cost of living increases to match the steadily rising cost of maintaining oneself with advanced age and the need for more than bare subsistence.

The adult children of these elders—many of whom are Baby Boomers—are now facing the task of trying to maintain their loved ones, help them stay safe, and at the same time provide for their own retirement needs. Some are also still raising their own children. They are often called "The Sandwich Generation," since they are caught between responsibilities for their own families at the same time as having to take on caregiving and financial responsibility for aging parents. It can be impossible to do all of these things well at the same time.

A consistent problem I see is that elders who lived through the Great Depression and have always been careful about money do not want to imagine their children ever having to do without as they did during those hard years. They saved money and want to leave a legacy, a gift to their offspring. Yet these same elders, who want very much to leave an inheritance to their children, may not appreciate that they actually need to spend their remaining funds just to live and pay for needed care. They may resist hiring help at home or allowing anyone to do so for them. To these elders, the hourly rate a caregiver charges seems much too expensive.

Their children may look forward to receiving an inheritance and may indeed feel entitled to it. This creates a conflict when the elder's needs for help exceed the elder's income. The carefully saved funds must be spent on home help, on assisted living, or even on a nursing home until the elder becomes impoverished. At that point, the elder will qualify for Medicaid, but the choices of where to live and how to manage are very limited.

Our country has simply not fully addressed the issue of aging and long-term care needs of our longest-living population. This leaves the family with pressure to figure it out or, in many cases, provide the needed care on their own.

THE SOLUTION: PLAN AHEAD YOURSELF, AND HELP YOUR AGING PARENTS PLAN RESPONSIBLY AS WELL

Most people do not like to think about getting old. Aging in our society has such a negative connotation; we seem to do everything we can to avoid thinking about or accepting it. We are inundated by the media with messages to "turn back the clock," "look and feel younger," and "fight aging" to the point that we probably think aging itself must be terrible. The effect of this barrage of negative messages is that we avoid considering our own aging, planning for it, and, most of all, facing that most of us are going to need some help in our later years if we live long lives.

The result of avoiding considering that we might get old and might need help as we do age is that we have no plan. Our parents have no plan. If they did have a plan, it did not extend to what would happen decades later when a modest pension was not enough to live on and Social Security could not cover the cost of living. An aging parent's health begins to falter, or they develop dementia, and no one quite knows what to do to cover the cost of caring for that parent. Some clients I meet have two impaired parents at once, doubling the size of the problem and their responsibility.

What can we do while our parents are still capable and competent to address the possibility that they will need care at some point? We need to educate ourselves, take proactive steps, and face the truth that care in any setting costs money, and the government is not going to pay for it unless you are at a poverty level. If there is no way our aging parent could pay for care, we need to address that and make our own plans accordingly.

THE PLANNING PROCESS

Educating yourself about what your aging loved ones currently need financially or may need in the future is the first step. Since we generally don't learn about how to manage our aging loved ones' later life issues in school, we have to study and research this topic on our own. If you start now, rather than waiting until there is a crisis, you will be better prepared to make the best decisions.

Evaluate Current Assets and Spending

In order to consider your aging parents' needs, you do need to know what they have in the bank, what income they receive, and what it costs them to live. This information can only be gathered if you ask your parents or other loved ones to talk it over with you. I've seen articles in elder-focused publications that suggest you need to have "The Talk" with your parents about money. I believe that it takes more than a single talk to do this job. It will require a series of conversations, best conducted where your aging loved ones are most comfortable and with advance warning that you need to go over these things with them. If you keep it relaxed and unpressured, you are likely to be more successful in getting the information you need to know to help them.

If you are not sure what questions to ask, we offer a "Family Security Planner" at AgingParents.com, available for purchase and downloadable. It has forms to help you cover all the things you need to ask about how to help you help your aging parent. In addition, it has legal forms, such as an Advance Healthcare Directive (a version specific to California) and a Durable Power of Attorney form, so you can get these documents in order during these conversations, if your parents do not already have these forms signed.

Generally, you need to know what assets your parents have, where they are kept, and how to access them. If your loved ones bank online, you will need passwords and account numbers.

One of the main reasons for getting this financial information is to enable you to figure out how your parents might pay for care if they needed it in the future. That is a very important question, since it could direct their actions and yours for years before such help might become necessary. Do they need to be more conservative about spending? Set aside funds each month? Plan to move in with family when help is needed? All these questions may come up.

You can record your parents' financial information electronically and keep it in a safe place, or you can print out various record-keeping forms, as we offer in the "Family Security Planner," and store them in a secure location. Any form of keeping this kind of information is fine. As long you are thorough and organized in gathering it, you are doing better than most. All too many adult children do not even venture into the area of discussing finances until a parent is hospitalized or in some other crisis. Then it may be very difficult or too late to get what you need.

The planning process should include using a trusted professional advisor to help you learn how to make the most of what your parent has and what you have. If there is money to invest, proper and competent financial advice can make a difference in how things turn out when a parent needs help. If there is nothing for your parent to invest—if they have nothing to spare other than the money they live on—you may need to seek advice yourself about how to either save money to help them later on, or get legal advice about how to get them qualified to receive public benefits, which we discuss further later in this chapter.

What If My Parent Resists Talking About Finances?

As we have discussed in previous chapters, it's not uncommon for our elders to refuse or resist the discussion you need to have about their money. To them, money may be a private matter, and they may consider it rude to ask. They may fear that you will take advantage of them or that they will lose control somehow if you know what they have. If they have very little, they may be embarrassed to tell you. Finances are an emotional and touchy subject for many. Respect that if your parents have traditionally been secretive about their finances.

You can meet their resistance in several ways. Many of the same principles apply to financial conversations that apply to getting help at home, giving up the car keys, or making other age-related adjustments. Discussing finances can be very emotional.

These are the highlights to remember:

- **Make it your problem, not theirs.**

- **Persist: you can accept your parents' refusal the first time, but let them know that you are going to bring it up again.**

- **Choose the right time and place.** Take advantage of a family gathering; if you are visiting your loved ones over a holiday, birthday, or special occasion, arrange to set aside extra time to stay over or arrive ahead to speak about finances.

- **Choose the right words.** You have to remain unemotional, even if the parent gets defensive or emotional. Practice saying the words—maybe in the mirror—that you think, knowing your parents, will not be threatening to them.

  For example, you might consider saying something like this:

  "Mom and Dad, I know this is not easy for you, but I need to have some information about your finances so that, if a health problem came up, I would be able to help you. Remember when Uncle Jack had his stroke, and he couldn't speak or make sense of things for a long time? If you had a health issue like that, I wouldn't know the first thing to do to keep your bills paid. Please help me out. I want to go over some basics so I'll feel better about any possible emergency you could have."

  Note in this example that you have made the issue your problem and not your parents' problem. You got to the point and used an example of a relative who did have a medical condition that was disabling. You asked for their help. You phrased it as being about an emergency, not about their potential general incapacity. It may be easier for them to have the "in case of emergency" conversation than to talk about dementia or losing capacity, though that could be your underlying concern, too.

- **Get help.** Parents may behave better in the presence of a neutral outsider.

Once You Know Your Parent's Financial Status, What Should You Do Next?

Your parents may not appreciate just how expensive it is to pay for care. They may not have any prior experience in hiring a home care worker or checking into the costs of assisted living or a nursing home. Doing the search for this kind of information may be up to you. There is plenty of research on the subject of the cost of long-term care. Some of it is funded by long-term care insurance providers because they want consumers to buy their long-term care insurance products. And, indeed, that may be a good idea if your parents can afford it. More on this subject of long-term care insurance is covered later in this chapter.

As we have discussed, one of the places to start exploring what resources exist in your parents' community is the Area Agency on Aging. These are federally funded offices that help residents of the county find and use services for elders. They may, for example, direct you to senior centers, transportation services, home health agencies, and social services for low-income elders. They can share handbooks, community directories, and online resources to help educate you about what services the county offers. Your Area Agency on Aging may be part of the county Health and Human Services Department, which is a part of local government.

If you have a parent who is in declining health and you have thought about the possibility of assisted living or board and care, you can find out about all the facilities in your parent's area online. Private, for-profit organizations exist to help direct you to all available facilities and to refer you to places that are within a desired price range. Be warned, however, that none of these profit-making organizations are set up specifically for low-income elders. If your aging loved ones have low income and will need care in the future—particularly help with activities of daily living, such as bathing and dressing—your choices are limited.

Leona's Move

Leona was only sixty-three when she suffered a massive stroke. Prior to that time, she had been supporting herself, living with her daughter in a comfortable apartment. She worked full time. Her daughter had just finished college and was searching for a good job when Leona suffered the devastating stroke. It took over a year for her to recover.

When she came out of rehabilitation, she needed a place to live, since her daughter had moved and had an apartment with a roommate.

Leona had only a small retirement fund and Social Security as income. She was not yet ready to return to work at age sixty-five, given some lingering effects of the stroke. She needed some help, but not nursing care. Assisted living cost twice what her income would cover. She used a board and care locator agency to find a local home that had a room for her within her price range. It was in a private home, and she was lucky enough to find one with a private bath. That solved her problem. But this kind of situation would only work for a person who did not need much in the way of daily help other than assistance with her medications. Leona can bathe and dress herself, walk independently, and her mind is clear. For a more infirm aging parent, the cost of care would likely exceed her income. A family member would have to help support her if she wanted to live outside a nursing home.

We often hear about aging parents who have only Social Security as income, which ranges from about $800–$1200 per month or may be even less. That is not enough to live on in most places. Add to that the cost of caregivers, and you can see why advance planning is necessary. We do not want our aging loved ones to become homeless. If they need help, we want them to have that help. We want to keep them safe.

Educate yourself about every possible benefit and

public program, and help your parents plan if it seems that they may qualify for a benefit.

UNDERSTAND AND MAKE USE OF PUBLIC BENEFITS

Most people who have not planned ahead have a belief that if they are older and do not have much money, the government will take care of them. That is only partly true. Benefits offered by the federal and state governments are very limited and do not cover everything elders need. One of the biggest myths is that Medicare, the federal health insurance program, will pay for long-term care at home. It does not pay for care at home, particularly the kind of custodial care we discussed in Chapter 7, "How to Choose a Home Care Worker." That is exactly the kind of care most aging people need to remain in their homes—help with shopping, bathing, meal preparation, dressing, and the like. It is not skilled nursing, and it is not covered by Medicare at all.

A lot of my clients are confused trying to distinguish between Medicare and Medicaid. This chapter is not meant to be a complete treatise on any kind of insurance, so my explanation will be very brief as to the distinction between these two government-sponsored programs. I am leaving out details in the interest of keeping the information as basic as possible. You can find out much more at the federal government's website, Medicare.gov, or your own state's website for Medicaid.

Medicare

Medicare is a federal program of health insurance. To receive this benefit, one must be sixty-five years old or totally disabled. The elder also must have paid into the system by having taxes taken out of one's paychecks and have applied for Medicare. One does not automatically start receiving it unless you apply. It includes a prescription drug benefit. You can apply for Medicare within a set time period before turning sixty-five or during an open enrollment period each year between mid-October and December 7. Your aging loved one should apply for Medicare, including the prescription drug benefit (Part D) as soon as they are eligible. If they do not apply for Part D as soon as they are eligible, there is a financial penalty for applying later.

Medicare covers 80 percent of health care costs for hospitalization and outpatient (doctor's office) visits. The other 20 percent is either covered by supplemental insurance, sometimes called "Medigap" insurance, or paid out of pocket. It is not a good idea to go without supplemental insurance. The 20 percent that Medicare does not cover can be extremely expensive to pay out-of-pocket, given the high cost of any medical treatment in this country.

Medicare requires payment of a monthly premium, which is automatically deducted out of the recipient's

Social Security check. The supplemental insurance is also paid with monthly premiums. There is a difference in the amount of the premium for people who make $80,000 or more per year as compared with Medicare recipients who make less. Otherwise, there is no income requirement for eligibility for Medicare.

Medicaid

Medicaid is an insurance plan for the lowest-income people in our society; it is paid with a combination of federal, state, and county funds. It is tied to the applicant's income and assets, not the individual's age. Any low-income person, depending on the state's requirements, can apply when eligible. It is regulated by each state, and each state has its own income and eligibility requirements. For example, in California you are eligible if you have no more than $2,000 in the bank (Though you can own a home and car, plus certain other cash assets and still qualify.).

The Centers for Medicare and Medicaid Services (CMS) regulates Medicaid and reviews what each state is doing. It has become progressively more aggressive about pursuing reimbursement to the state when a person does have a home and has received Medicaid. For example, if your aging parent owns a home, but has no cash in the bank and applies for Medicaid to pay for a nursing home, she may indeed receive Medicaid. However, you, as the potential heirs, may have to pay Medicaid back for the cost of care out of the sale of the home after your mother passes.

For low-income "dual eligibles" who receive both Medicare and Medicaid, Medicaid pays for the other 20 percent of the cost of care that Medicare does not cover. In other words, the elder who gets Medicaid no longer has to pay out-of-pocket for supplemental or Medigap insurance.

Besides paying for 20 percent of what Medicare does not cover, Medicaid is the only public insurance program that pays for long-term care in nursing homes. Although no one would likely pick a nursing home as the first choice for where to live, it is the only choice for many low-income elders who are frail enough to need long-term nursing care.

In addition, in some communities in some states, Medicaid-eligible people can also qualify for limited help at home. In my state of California, for example, the program is called In Home Supportive Services. It is supported by state and county funding, and it will cover hourly payments to home care workers who take care of a person who is able to remain at home. The eligible person may have medical conditions not so severe that skilled nursing is required each day. Relatives can apply to be home care workers for their dependent loved one, which can help offset the sacrifice they make in taking care of a loved one themselves. Otherwise, outside workers come in and provide the care. The state and county reimbursement to the workers is less than an employee would earn working at a care facility. The hours are limited, and these programs do not allow for 24/7 care that would otherwise be given in a nursing home.

Not Eligible?

Suppose your aging parents have enough income and money in the bank that they are not eligible for Medicaid, but you are worried about what will happen if they live a long time and run out of savings. In that situation, it is very important to seek competent legal advice about when your aging loved one could become eligible for Medicaid. It is tricky, and the rules can be changed by the state legislature any time. If you have concerns about your parents' long-term financial situation, I suggest that you get advice in your parents' state about what requirements they would have to meet to become eligible. Planning years in advance is prudent because the CMS regulators will look back at all financial transactions, such as selling or giving away a home or other assets for a period of five years prior to the application in many states. Above all, do not think that if you just move assets out of your parent's name, you can trick the state into thinking that they are poor enough to qualify for this benefit. Your parent has to present all financial information on the application, and falsifying it, or fraud, is a crime.

Veteran's Benefits

A less-known, possible source of payment for long-term care is called Aid and Attendance under the Veteran's Administration (VA) of the federal government. This program is for vets and their spouses. It can be very helpful in paying for part of the cost of care at home or in assisted living. An elderly vet, for example, who needs help with bathing, dressing, and walking, and who qualifies on the basis of income can receive as much as $2,054 a month in cash payments.

All of the information about VA benefits, such as Aid and Attendance, is available for free at the Department of Veteran's Affairs website, http://veteranaid.org/eligibilit/php. One should never pay for information or counseling about how to get VA benefits because the government wants the public to have it. It is always free to find out about the benefit and how to access it from published government sources. However, legal advice may be needed to help with the application and eligibility. An attorney who has special knowledge and experience in VA and Medicaid eligibility should be consulted for questions about what your loved one needs to do to become eligible for Aid and Attendance.

A word of warning: Beware of organizations that offer free lunches or dinners for those who want to get VA Aid and Attendance. Some are merely a cover for organizations hoping to get elders' financial information in order to sell them inappropriate investments.

Subsidized Senior Housing

Another resource to look into for low-income aging parents or other relatives is called subsidized housing for elders and persons with disabilities. It offers special programs that allow a low-income elder (or disabled person) who meets eligibility criteria to live in an apartment within the program at a specific location at a reduced rent. These subsidized apartments become part of these affordable rent programs when the apartment owner applies for and is accepted to offer apartments to qualified tenants. The rent in these housing programs is calculated at about one third of the resident's income. In other words, if your aging parent needs housing and can't afford market rents, you may wish to explore the possibility of a reduced rent apartment. For example, if she has about $1,000 a month from Social Security and that is all she has, her rent in a federally subsidized apartment in the program would be about $330. The federal government makes up the difference between the rent paid and the cost of the apartment.

The federal government sponsors these projects throughout the United States. Information can be found on the Department of Housing and Urban Development (HUD) website at www.Portal.HUD.gov; however, the website is not updated often, so the information there could well be out of date. Your parents' local housing authority or similar county government agency may have a current list of available subsidized senior housing nearby.

There are different kinds of programs for low-income families than for those designated particularly for seniors and disabled persons. If your aging loved one is running low on money and can't afford to pay for a home or a market rate apartment, there are at least some possible options that would allow him to live independently, even if he has very little coming in each month. Some seniors run low on cash and sell the family home, tapping their only resource to live on the proceeds. Little by little, money from the sale is spent on another living arrangement and ordinary expenses of daily life. When a person lives long enough, that cash may be depleted as well. This creates a major crisis.

One way to avert this financial disaster is, once again, to plan ahead. Help your loved one calculate the cost of living and how long his savings and proceeds from selling the family home will last. You can help your loved one pay rent or support the rent entirely, or apply for seniors' subsidized housing. One drawback is that subsidized housing is independent living. If your parent is frail and in need of help, that help is not available as a part of sub-sidized housing. There may be activities and some limited services onsite in seniors' housing, but the resident must either be able to live independently or hire help to manage the activities of daily living that he can't handle by himself. We must distinguish independent living from assisted living. The HUD programs are not for assisted living apartments. They do, however, offer accommodation for wheelchairs and other adaptive aids.

Be aware that it may be extremely difficult to get subsidized housing in popular areas to live, since the demand far exceeds the supply. There are many more needy seniors who qualify for subsidized housing than there are apartments available. Some of the units may not be in safe or desirable neighborhoods, and some may not be convenient or in a location your parent knows well. Some have waitlists as long as seven to ten years. Some have such long waiting lists that a senior can't even apply to be on the list. If you think there is a possibility that your loved one will run out of funds to live on, it makes sense to apply for available housing as soon as possible, in hopes that his name will come up on the wait list by the time his cash to pay rent elsewhere is depleted.

Private Insurance

Some clients have the mistaken belief that, if they have good health insurance from a large insurer, then it will pay for long-term care for their aging parent. Health insurance does not typically pay for long-term care. It may pay for short-term care at home, just as Medicare does. That would mean that the elder requires a licensed nurse or therapist for a limited time to come into the home and do treatment or therapy. A few visits would be paid for, and then Medicare or the private coverage would stop.

The only kind of private insurance that does cover

long-term care is called long-term care insurance (LTCi). According to the National Bureau of Economic Research, only about 10 percent of Americans have this kind of insurance.[1] That means that, for 90 percent of Americans, the cost of caring for our elders is borne out-of-pocket or is paid for directly by family.

If it covers the kind of care so many people need, why don't more people buy it? There are probably many reasons why we avoid this kind of insurance, the most obvious of which is the cost. Customers must pay into a policy for years, and over decades it adds up to thousands and thousands of dollars. It is more expensive if you wait to buy it until you are a senior, even if you are in good health. And, unlike other health insurance—which, under the Affordable Care Act, cannot refuse you because of a pre-existing condition—long-term care insurers can refuse you for prior health conditions. And they do decline coverage or charge exorbitantly high prices for premiums if you have certain health issues. If your loved one has dementia, for example, forget trying to get long-term care insurance. Carriers will refuse them. If they have had recent surgery, have rheumatoid arthritis, insulin-dependent diabetes, or a host of other risky conditions, the carriers see them as an unprofitable prospect and do not want to provide coverage. If coverage is offered at all, the price may be too high to consider.

Another reason many people do not seek out this kind of coverage is because they cannot imagine that they will ever need it. It goes back to our negative images of aging and how we avoid thinking about getting old. We ignore it and live in the fantasy that we will always be able to care for ourselves independently. Then, if a health condition arises that would make long-term care insurance a good thing, it is too late.

I had to consider this question, myself, before I turned sixty—an age when premiums go up. My husband and I discussed it at length, and I did my research. I talked to a knowledgeable broker whom I trusted. I knew about long-term care from personal experience. And I ended up buying a policy for myself and my husband. To put it simply, we did the math. We looked at the cost of premiums for both of us with the couples' discount and added the premium payments from the date of purchase until age eighty-five. I chose eighty-five because that was about the age when my grandmother needed help. I looked at what the benefit would pay out to me if I were to require home help three times a week for four hours a day from age eighty-five to age one hundred. I could see in my analysis that my investment in premiums was a lot less than the potential payout. So, we took the chance to insure against risk.

And things have changed since then. Premiums have increased significantly for those who have not yet bought long-term care insurance. Single women, in particular, are charged more for coverage because the insurance carriers consider them a higher risk. While women in general pay higher premiums than men, single women pay even more than married women.

One reason women are hit particularly hard with high premiums is that women usually take care of their husbands, who then don't have to make a claim under their long-term care insurance policies. Then the women outlive their husbands and have no one to take care of them. Of course more women will need to access benefits because of this.

For many, the cost of this kind of insurance just isn't worth it in their minds, and they have a point. Ninety percent of people believe the insurance is not worth the premiums. Obviously, we have no idea if we will live to be one hundred or if we will need help. We do not know if we will ever collect on the policy. I have met a ninety-year-old in assisted living who had long-term care insurance and could not get any benefits, despite paid up premiums, because she did not meet the stringent criteria her policy required that she meet before she could get anything from the insurance company. I know others who are collecting premiums and are so grateful that they bought the insurance. It pays for help at home or in assisted living.

I also know a ninety-three-year-old who purchased a comprehensive, long-term care policy and needs full-time care to the extent of the coverage he purchased. And his awful company, which has been sued in a class action lawsuit for unfair claims practices, continues to treat him badly and tries repeatedly to get out of paying what is rightfully his. Every time he battles them, he gets his benefits reinstated, but it is a battle that recurs over and over as the insurer tries to find excuses to drop him.

Another issue to consider is the sustainability of the LTCi industry. It is not clear if the long-term care insurance industry, which is losing ground in the numbers of insured, is even going to survive when it has to pay out millions more in claims for all those who are living to be one hundred and collecting benefits. The prospects for the future may be fine, but some consider them controversial.

What's the takeaway here? There are consumer risks; be aware of these. Policies are expensive, no one knows how long she or he will live, and there are problems with companies honoring the benefits. However, if your parents are young enough that carriers of this kind of insurance are offering reasonable prices for premiums—because it's cheaper when your parent is younger and healthy—find out the details. Research what policies are available to them. There are good companies and policies out there, and this insurance could, in the end, save your loved one and you thousands of dollars.

- Consider it.

- Calculate the cost.

- Explore options.

- Discuss.

Talk about the prospect with them and see what they think, too. Fill out an application and get a quote. Without such insurance, the burden of caring for aging loved ones could fall directly on you. Are you prepared for that possibility? Think it through. If the cost of the premiums is just too high, then you must figure out a way to pay for long-term care yourself or save a lot of money ahead of time in case care is needed. Remember that if your loved one needs care, someone has to pay for it. If the family cannot afford to save for care or pay for it themselves, the other option is to take in your elder and help provide care yourself. Many families do this, sometimes at great personal sacrifice. Taking in an aging parent affects every member of the family. It works well in some families and is disastrous in others.

A colleague of mine, who is financially comfortable, lives alone. She is in her early fifties, divorced, and has two grown children. She does not want to have her sons burdened with care for her if she needs it in her future. Her financial advisor suggested that she get long-term care insurance. Currently, she is an exceptionally strong triathlete in excellent health. But she is smart enough to see that she may not be fit and strong until her dying day, and she took a step to be sure she can pay for long-term care if she needs it some decades down the road. She has the resources to pay for the premiums, even though the pricing is gender-based and seems unfair to women. She bought it anyway.

If you are wondering how much care actually costs, here is some information you may find surprising. Be sure you understand what risk you are actually taking if you do not have insurance or adequate savings.

Know the Cost of Long-Term Care

According to the Alzheimer's Association report[2], which comes out annually, the average cost of a paid, unlicensed caregiver with some training who provides non-medical care is $21 per hour or $168 per day. Could your aging parents afford that, and if so, for how long?

An option to help elders who need some care during the day, especially if they have memory loss issues or dementia, is adult day service or adult day health service. The concept is like day care, in that the elder goes to a location where safety, supervision, and activities are offered, sometimes with licensed nursing supervision. Those places that offer nursing supervision often use the term "day health," while others that do not offer nursing supervision may use other terminology, such as "day services." They avoid the term "day care," which typically applies only to children. These are a great help to working families with elders in need of care during the workday. The average cost of adult day services was $70 per day, with higher charges in some centers for people with dementia.

Assisted living facilities are an option for long-term care for some, but it is not suitable for everyone. The average annual cost of basic assisted living services was $42,000 per year. For facilities that charge a higher rate for dementia care, the annual cost was $57,684. As we discussed in the earlier section on assisted living, the cost is much higher in states where the overall cost of housing is much higher than average.

Imagine that your loved one needs nursing home care and is not eligible yet for Medicaid. After the maximum of one hundred days when Medicare coverage runs out, the average cost of a semi-private room in a nursing home was $222 per day, or $81,830 per year. Could your aging parent afford that?

Legal Issues

In some states, there are old laws on the books called "filial support laws." These require that adult children, if financially capable, must pay for the cost of nursing home care for a parent. There are about thirty states with these laws, but they are not enforced everywhere. However, some high profile lawsuits by nursing homes against adult children have been successful. How can a family member protect against such a lawsuit?

There are some important steps to take which should protect you:

First, if your aging parent is likely to be eligible for Medicaid, get the application done as soon as possible. Medicaid would prevent any nursing home from having a claim against an adult child for an unpaid nursing home bill. If your aging loved one must go to a nursing home and he is already eligible for Medicaid, be sure the facility accepts Medicaid. Not all do. Make certain that your loved one has any help he needs with the application process. It can be difficult for an older person. The application form is likely available online in your parent's state, and you can download and fill it out for her, as well as supply all the requested documents needed to prove eligibility.

Second, never sign any document, contract, or other agreement with a facility that makes *you* the responsible person for payment. This paperwork may call you an agent, representative, or any other wording they want to use. Do not be confused if you are your parent's agent on a Durable Power of Attorney. Even if you are, you are still not the recipient of care. An agent on the DPOA is not responsible for covering the parent's bills from his own pocket. You, as an agent, are simply acting on behalf of your parent to pay bills with whatever resources your parent has. You didn't sign on to pay for his care out of your own pocket when you agreed to serve as an agent on a DPOA.

Your parent is the responsible person, whether he has Medicaid or not. He is a party to the contract, not you, since you get no benefit from the contract. You may get pressured or told things that are untrue to get you to sign as the responsible person. Don't sign unless you agree to pay the bill yourself if necessary. This applies to nursing homes, assisted living facilities, and board and care homes.

You are not the recipient of service, and you are not responsible for paying for the services unless you choose to do so.

Finally, do not place your aging loved one in any facility she cannot afford. If she starts out doing fairly well and later develops symptoms of dementia, she may have to move to a "memory care" part of a care facility. The cost there will be higher. If she needs the care and can afford to pay for it, there is no problem. But if she can't afford the higher cost unit, it is better to plan for a move to a place she can afford. Some family members have expressed disbelief that a loved one is being asked to move out of assisted living when she runs out of financial resources. I am not sure what they were expecting. These places are largely for-profit institutions. They do not have any loyalty to a person who can't afford the care. They are a business and need to fill every bed or room with a paying resident.

SUMMARY

Given the high cost of long-term care, it is not surprising that many families have to help their aging loved ones. People are living long enough to run out of money, and this creates a financial burden few have anticipated. The best protection you have if you are concerned that your parents may not have enough to live on as they age is to plan ahead while they are still able to manage on their own for their financial future.

Good planning can help your aging parents access

every available public benefit for which they may be eligible. If they can qualify for Medicaid, subsidized housing, Veterans' Aid and Attendance, or any other community resource where they live, they may have a much safer and more secure future. If they will not likely qualify, it is important for you to do some good advance planning so that you will not be caught off guard if the need to help them financially does come up.

TAKING YOUR AGING PARENT INTO YOUR HOME

As you look at the high cost of care, you can fully understand why millions of Americans are giving their loved ones long-term care at home themselves. There are simply no other affordable options for most families. We don't get to set life's clock. We don't know if or when we may need help. But looking at what most people need, we can conclude that our aging parents will likely need care in some form before the end of their lives.

You need to be ready for this reality. You should discuss, as a family, who would and could help their aging parents or other loved ones when help is needed. The history of our country included caring for our own at home as they aged. This was at a time when families often lived in multi-generation households. Now, families may be scattered across the country or across the world. The question of who is willing and able to care for an aging parent who can't manage alone must be addressed.

Caring for an aging loved one at home is a unique challenge, particularly when the elder must move to be with family, or a family member must move in with an aging parent or grandparent. Enormous adjustments must be made. Some families make an effort to share the responsibility, while others unfairly expect that a daughter will do the job just because she is the daughter. Others simply ignore a parent's care needs, leaving the burden of doing the work on the sibling who lives closest geographically.

BASIC SAFEGUARDS

There is no single solution to the question of how to best care for an aging parent who needs help and cannot be alone any longer. There are, however, some basic safeguards every family should take to avoid nasty conflicts over this issue. Family fights about caring for an aging parent can spin out of control, end up in court, or continue for years—even after a parent passes away.

Safeguard #1: Make a Plan

Discuss among all family members, near and far, that a plan needs to be in place for possible caregiving if a parent needs it. As a personal example, a member of my family is a stroke victim, and he needs to be in a care facility. He has no money, and his income is Social Security. When he needed to move out of a nursing home, the family had to come together to make a decision. Where was he going to go? My family has always struggled to have healthy communication, and some members tend to clash. It is often hard to work together in harmony, so coming together in any way was difficult.

There were arguments over whether our family member could live in his apartment alone after his stroke.

There were disagreements over how he would afford assisted living if it turned out to be the best option.

In spite of all the conflict, the family agreed to share the cost of assisted living for him, so he could have a dignified existence in an apartment with the supervision he needed. We formed a plan, and he moved in and is doing very well to this day. Even in families that do not get along, like mine, it is possible to form plans and make agreements.

If your loved one is in declining health, the time to start planning is not after a crisis—it is right now. The logistics of care should be talked over. The amount of time a person puts into the effort of caregiving tends to increase as the elder grows older, and the change needs to be discussed. What is fair? How can the family equalize the burden? What can those who live far away do to contribute? How much can they visit? What can the aging parent do for the caregiving family members? Provide a place to live? Make payments? Give a larger share of any inheritance? These topics should not be avoided.

Safeguard #2: Create Caregiver Contracts

Some of the ugliest fights in families arise from failure to consider the value of an adult child's service to the elder who needs care. As you can see from this chapter, the cost of having an outside person or facility provide care is very expensive. When family members step in and do this work, it has a dollar value, whether the elder can actually afford to pay it or not. The value is a source of contention, as some family members fail to recognize the value or discount it. The person doing the caregiving, however, knows that doing so requires more than love for the elder. It often also requires financial sacrifice. Caregiving adult children may have to quit their jobs to take care of an aging parent. They may lose benefits from work and sacrifice contributions to their own retirement plan. Taking an aging parent in causes a ripple effect and strain on other family members in the household.

When there are siblings who are not providing any physical care, and the bulk of responsibility falls on one sibling, this is a recipe for resentment and family conflict, if not warfare. A good way to prevent this is by the use of a caregiver contract.

The contract is suitable when there is any asset available to compensate the family caregiver for the sacrifice and labor involved in caregiving. Usually that means the elder's home or personal property of value. A lawyer who is familiar with these issues can draw up such a contract for the family and describe in it how there is something of value to be given to the primary caregiver in exchange for the work of caregiving.

It does not have to be elaborate to be helpful. Basically, the person doing the primary caregiving work gets something in return for doing so. The other family members sign on and make this agreement official. For example, after the elder passes away, the primary caregiver might inherit more than the others or get the family home or a larger share of any other asset available. The terms depend on what the elder who needs care has to give, as well as what the caregiver and the rest of the family find acceptable. With the help of a lawyer who may be able to remain more neutral than the family members involved, the family can protect itself from deep-seated resentments that can fester for years and destroy relationships.

This is one device that can work. Other families are able to work out less formal agreements and do well enough. But the danger of doing nothing can easily lead to a great deal of anger and damage to the family.

If you have an aging loved one, consider that some person in the family will have to take on responsibility that could be disproportionate to what others do. Aim for fairness. Recognize that caregiving for anyone is work. The more complex the diagnoses the elder has, the more work the caregiver has to do. An elder with Alzheimer's disease, for example, can become a 24/7 job, and there is no way to keep the elder safe without considerable vigilance. Consider also that full-time family caregivers often develop health problems of their own. Their sacrifice must be recognized.

Rachel's Story

Rachel was named as the agent on the DPOA and advance healthcare directives for three elderly relatives. She had no siblings and took on the task willingly, but with some fear that it might be too much. Eventually all three of her elders were placed in an assisted living facility. She found that to be convenient when she visited, but, as time went on, their needs increased. She was taking one or the other of them in a wheelchair to the doctor every week, and, because of incontinence, she was doing four loads of laundry each day. The assisted living facility only provided laundry service once a week. She came to me asking for some advice about what to do. We made an appointment, but she was not able to keep it. She was hospitalized with a heart attack.

Rachel had to rely on a geriatric care manager and another distant relative while she recuperated. I advised her to keep using the care manager to take some of the burden off herself, which worked. It had never dawned on her that the relentless stress of her caregiver responsibilities was ruining her own health. After the sobering event of her hospitalization, she began to appreciate herself more. Caregiver stress is a constant for many, as it was for Rachel. This is a factor that should be figured into the cost of care when your family considers a plan for taking care of your aging loved ones.

FAMILIES WHO SHARE THE WORK OF CAREGIVING

Different cultures in our society view the issue of aging parents differently. Asian families, Latino families, and others may generally consider it their own responsibility to care for an aging loved one themselves, rather than expecting to have their loved one go to a costly care facility. I met one Filipino family with two aging and impaired parents who needed a lot of help at home. They had several daughters, who took turns leaving everything to come and take care of their parents. One flew in from the Philippines, leaving her job, her husband, and her children to relieve her other sister, who had quit her own job for two months to care for these parents. This arrangement worked for them, since their parents had low income and the daughters considered it an expectation that they would need to do this at some time in their lives.

Another large family had a grandmother in her nineties who could not manage alone. They took turns moving the grandmother around from one relative to another, each taking her in for a period of months, so that no one had to handle the responsibility for an unspecified amount of time.

Another family I met had four generations under the same roof. All took some responsibility caring for their aging grandmother or great-grandmother. This seemed to work well also. Every family is different, and cultural expectations have a strong influence on how things are worked out. None of these families had a lot of money to spare or spend on paid caregivers, at least not full time. All of them had to work together to help each other with the responsibilities involved. They talked it over and decided who would and could do what. That is more ideal than many people might find in their own families. The communication about how to help care for aging parents who do not have money is a critical piece here and essential if caregiving is something aging parents can't afford to pay for themselves.

ADULT CHILDREN WHO SUPPORT THEIR PARENTS

I have also met plenty of adult children who support their aging parents financially, almost completely or as a supplement to a parent's modest income. If the adult children are doing well financially and can afford the rather steep cost of helping and purchasing caregiving for their parents, they generously offer to do so. There are often conflicts about this arrangement, however, as siblings rarely all have the same financial capability. One who has financial success may resent being burdened with paying all or most of the cost to support an aging relative, while the other sibling or siblings do relatively little.

I encourage discussion about this to head off family conflicts about the disproportionate burden. If one can provide financial support, perhaps another can do other chores, such as managing medication, trips to the doctor, or household maintenance. The worst approach is to simply ignore the reality that a low-income parent needs help and that someone has to help. Resentment becomes toxic as the family fails to openly discuss what each person needs, wants, and is capable of doing. If you see yourself in this situation of potential resentment about an aging parent's support for any reason, be the leader and bring it up with your siblings or other relatives—talk it out. It can make a great deal of difference in how things are handled when the time comes that help is needed.

A LEGAL NOTE FOR CAREGIVERS

If you must take time off from work to take care of an aging family member, the federal government ensures that, under certain circumstances, some employees may take leave from their jobs without having to lose their employment.

The law that provides this is called the Family and Medical Leave Act (FMLA).[1] It is administered through the US Department of Labor.

The law provides that certain employees can take up to twelve weeks of unpaid, job-protected leave per year. It also requires that their group health benefits be maintained during the leave. FMLA applies to all public agencies, all public and private elementary and secondary schools, and companies with fifty or more employees. You have to be with the employer at least twelve months and have worked at least 1,250 hours over the past twelve months to become eligible to take this leave. You must also work at a location where the company employs fifty or more employees within seventy-five miles.

One of my clients suddenly had to care for her mother when her father went into the hospital. She had been with her company for several years, and it was a large employer, so she met the requirements. At my suggestion, she went to the Human Resources department at her company and asked for the FMLA application. She filled it out, giving the reasons for her request for leave time. Her father's doctor filled out a form verifying that he had a serious medical condition. She also had to provide her mother's diagnosis, which was also a serious medical condition. She got her leave, and her job was protected for the three months she spent helping both of them. Leave was unpaid, but at least she had a job to go back to when things settled down with her parents.

SUMMARY

Many parents are without the means to provide for themselves, since they often live longer than they expected to live, particularly if they are infirm in any way. The work of caregiving may fall on their children if the parents can't afford the costs of living or the need for paid caregivers.

If your parents have low income, you may need to provide at least some of their care yourself, assuming it is needed at some point. If you can coordinate with your family to share the work of caregiving among relatives, you are in the best situation you can create.

Some adult children plan ahead to take in an aging parent and accommodate the need for space, helping with daily care and monitoring of their loved one, and they are able to make it work. Others may move the aging person from place to place so that all siblings share the tasks involved at different locations. The elder is the only one moving in those instances. Others have multiple generations all under one roof with various family members each doing part of the care. Others may move into the aging parent's home and give the care there. Since every family is different, and personalities do not always harmonize as we wish they would, each family must figure out the best path forward.

Above all, aim for fairness so that no one is left with too much responsibility when others can also help out.

It can really help to discuss what might happen in the

future when your parents are still independent and competent. It is never too early. They probably have preferences. Honor them when you can. Ask them what they would like to do if they needed help and there was not enough money available to hire helpers. Then, plan accordingly, taking every prudent step you can to ensure that you keep your loved ones safe in their declining years.

HOW TO CHOOSE A
HOME
CARE
WORKER

When an aging parent or other loved one starts to lose the ability to do everyday things alone—such as bathing or cooking—the elder or her family may consider getting a helper. Your parent may resist the idea of help initially. For some elders, having to rely on a helper for anything is stressful and threatening. It can have a symbolic meaning that they are "going downhill" or becoming a burden. Many elders fight against getting a helper, which they see as having a stranger in their house.

However, when the effects of aging prevent a loved one from managing her daily life alone, it is time to find out if help at home can solve the problem. The arena of home care workers is largely unregulated by government and by society in general. It is usually considered a private matter. The difficulty is that many people hire someone to work in the home without appreciating the hidden risks.

This chapter is an effort to educate adult children of aging parents, or the parents themselves, about known risks in hiring home care workers. We want to assist you through the hiring process and give you confidence through knowing what to expect and how to avoid the mistakes others have made.

GETTING HELP AT HOME

If you have noticed that your aging loved one is not managing so well on her own, you are probably considering getting help at home. As time passes, people begin to demonstrate some of the signs of aging, which include loss of physical strength, memory difficulty, and the inability to keep track of things. The combination of these problems—which may or may not include disease processes such as dementia, arthritis, and other ailments—may result in a decline in independence.

It is certainly a common trait that the elder herself is not the first to recognize a decline in independence. It seems to be something we naturally resist. We do not want to admit that we cannot be completely on our own or that we are not as capable as we used to be. To do so would be to recognize that we are getting closer to the end of our lives, and that acknowledgment is not something our society accepts.

Resistance to recognizing the need for help often comes from the elder, but sometimes the family members also resist recognizing an elder's decline. Facing the decline means facing that Mom or Dad is getting old, could be in failing health, and may die sooner rather than later. No one likes to deal with this, but the head-in-the-sand approach can lead to disaster.

Perhaps, on your last visit to your aging parents, you discovered that the house, which was always neatly kept, has been neglected. The yard has not been tended to, nor the grass mowed. Mom's clothes are dirty, and she was always very fastidious. There is not much food in the house. Prescription medicine bottles are in disorder, and some are empty. You may have been worrying about this for some time, and you have finally come to the conclusion that it is time to approach your aging loved ones with the subject of getting help.

Unfortunately, many people are in crisis when they finally start looking for a home care worker. If you are a responsible relative, it is not smart to wait until your loved one falls at home and gets hospitalized, or until you get a frantic call from a neighbor about your loved one. With some guidelines in mind, you can do the best job possible of finding a homecare worker and prevent the disasters that come from lack of planning.

Recommendations for Choosing a Home Care Worker

The following are recommendations as to what you can do to be a good consumer.

1. Spend some time doing research about how to locate the best caregiving resource.

Inadequate research and preparation can lead to placing an incompetent worker in a loved one's home, financial abuse or related criminal activity, and even physical assault. It may take you several hours to look into agencies or other resources in your community or the community where your aging loved ones reside. Most agencies have websites. Talk to at least a few agencies if you wish to go through an agency to hire a home care worker. Check local listings if you wish to do the hiring on your own. The pros and cons of going to an agency versus hiring someone on your own are discussed below.

2. Be involved.

If you live out of the area where your loved one resides, hire a geriatric care manager to assist you. If you do not have the means to hire a geriatric care manager to assist you, look for an agency which is very communicative and offers care management as a part of the services.

Some agency managers have no contact with the family or client's family after the worker is placed. Other agencies have frequent contact with the client's family, the physician, social worker, and other involved persons in a team approach. Ask about the agency's policy of being involved with the family of the elder after a worker is placed in the home.

3. Be sure to inquire about what kind of background and qualifications check, drug screening, and training is done by the agency before workers are hired.

Find out how much oversight and supervision the agency provides to its workers. Inquire about the frequency and method of communication with you, the person who is requesting placement of a worker in the home. Find out how long the agency has been in business, whether it is insured, and how many people are in charge of administration.

4. Be sure a thorough and professional needs assessment is done at the time a home worker is placed to assist your aging loved one.

Many agencies use an assessment tool, such as a checklist or questionnaire. Take a look at it, and ask to see the paperwork. Find out who does the assessment and their qualifications and experience in doing so.

5. Involve the elder as much as possible in the entire process.

If your aging loved one has limited mental capacity due to Alzheimer's disease or other dementia or conditions, their participation may be limited. However, persons in the earlier stages of dementia are still capable of participating, voicing an opinion, and providing their input. Generally, it is a mistake to simply march in and tell your aging parent what is going to happen. No one wants to lose a feeling of control over one's life. This is a critical issue.

If your loved one's mental status will allow, ask them to express their wishes, preferences, likes, and dislikes.

If your elder is resistant to the idea of placing someone in his or her home, be sure that you discuss it thoroughly and well in advance of bringing an agency representative or care manager into the home. Even if your loved one refuses to choose or give an opinion, make the effort to ask him to do so before choosing for the elder. If your elder's judgment is impaired and he is not able to use good judgment, work on choosing what you think he might like based on past history, behavior patterns, personality, etc.

6. Do a thorough safety inspection of the elder's home before a worker is placed there.

Everything from removing throw rugs to reconstructing bathrooms and building ramps should be considered, depending on what the elder needs. Remaining in the home is almost always the first choice, but it is not always the best choice.

An elder may not be safe at home. Just because he says, "I'll never go to one of 'those places for old people,'" does not mean it will not be necessary at some point. The deciding factor should be the elder's capability to remain at home with help, while not endangering the elder.

IF I GO WITH AN AGENCY, WHAT SHOULD I LOOK FOR?

An agency should be well established and should be able to provide you with references. It should have a written contract or price list spelling out the charges involved and the kinds of services it can provide. If you are not sure about signing a contract, you may have it reviewed by a lawyer. However, most of the things home care agencies provide are non-medical, common-sense services. It is not necessary to seek legal advice to review a service contract of this kind, unless there is any part of it about which you are confused or the agency is unable to answer your questions. If you have any doubt, seek legal advice.

The agency should provide a thorough assessment of your elder's needs at the outset. This should include a general assessment of the elder's physical, emotional, and psychosocial needs, as well as a review of the physical environment. Safety should also be one of the major concerns the agency has as a priority.

Following an assessment, the agency should give you suggestions as to what the elder's needs are as the agency has assessed them. You should be able to expect input from an agency, since their representative may be able to see things you have missed or that the elder has not told you about.

The agency should communicate with the elder's adult children or other relatives about the frequency and amount of home care they believe the elder needs. Many agency representatives have years of experience doing such assessments, and they can be quite helpful to you, the consumer, in making suggestions. Family members may not have a clear understanding of what the elder's needs really are. This comes from the fact that the elder may not live with their adult children, that the elder may not clearly describe the problems he is having, and the fact that the elder's needs are probably changing as time goes by.

WHAT IF THE ELDER IS RESISTANT TO IN-HOME HELP?

Working through the elder's resistance is the first step. You must respect the elder, yet gently push ahead, presenting the idea of help for the sake of the peace of mind of the adult child. The elder may agree to try it. You and your family may be able to persuade the elder to accept some help by describing that you need to have more peace of mind while at work or with your own families, or because you live out of the area.

Once help is in place, you have a better chance that the elder will not reject the person who regularly comes to offer assistance. If the worker shows up each time with a kindly, respectful attitude and asks the elder what he would like, it can induce the elder to stick with having this help. Again, helping the elder maintain a sense of control is very important.

Elders will often tell us, "I've been doing fine all by myself, and I don't need any help." No one seems to be quite ready to believe that he or she needs assistance with ordinary things. However, acknowledging and honoring the elder's belief in his own independence, while reminding him that the adult relative or child needs reassurance that the elder is safe, can be a good approach.

Five Siblings and Two Difficult Parents

A large family, with five adult children, was in a quandary about both their parents, since both parents had dementia in its earlier stages. The children had to get together for a massive and complex undertaking of getting both parents to make some major changes. One of the changes involved getting a worker to help them and to drive them around. There was absolute refusal at first. When the parents lost the ability to drive, their children seized the opportunity to all get together with the parents and to hire a home care worker. In this case, the parents refused to be involved in the decision about which worker to hire because they did not think they needed help. So, their children did the research and found a kindly woman who was tough enough to deal with a few cross—even abusive—words at the beginning.

The children met their parents for a special occasion and took them out for a meal. When they returned, they had arranged for the home care worker to come to the home to meet the parents. The kids had told their parents at the luncheon about the worker, and the parents, of course, said they didn't need help. The children said it was just for driving, to start. Since the parents had no choice about that, they accepted it on a temporary basis. One of the sons stayed overnight to help with the adjustment and to explain to the worker the next day what his parents needed. The worker offered to prepare a meal and do a few chores, and the parents began to reluctantly accept this.

There were continued refusals and bumps in the process, but the worker was steady, patient, and just kept showing up. The parents eventually grew to rely on her and even like her. This was one success story with teamwork and planning being the largest elements contributing to the transition.

WHAT ARE THE ADVANTAGES AND DISADVANTAGES OF HIRING A HOME WORKER ON YOUR OWN?

Advantages

It is possible to hire a qualified and good home care worker on your own without going through an agency. The main advantage is that you will save money. The home care business is a profit-making business, and the people who are sending workers into individual homes need to make a profit in order to stay viable. They will charge more, in most cases, than you will pay if you do not use an agency. We recommend that you always use an agency to place a worker in your home if you can afford it. We believe that the risks are not worth the relatively small cost difference of going through a reputable agency to get a competent worker to help your elder at home.

Disadvantages

There are many disadvantages to hiring someone on your own. They include these things:

1. You may not have the resources or knowledge to do a thorough drug or other screening and criminal background check.

Agencies may contract for these services at a reduced rate. An individual will have to spend money out of pocket, find a good background checking service, and get the information coming from the background check before hiring a helper. Without an agency, you have to do all the screening yourself. You must call references, search public records, and conduct more than one interview. The process can be daunting.

2. You may not have experience in screening and hiring people to do work in the home.

This can be a disadvantage. People who are looking for this kind of work as a way of finding an opportunity to commit elder financial abuse may present very well, and may be congenial, experienced, and warm. It is much easier to be fooled by this if you are hiring someone for the first time than if you hire people as a part of your daily business. Experienced agency employers may have developed a nose for the unsuitable worker. It could be that you, as an individual trying to hire on your own, lack the sophistication and skill to hire with intelligence.

3. The risk of theft.

Theft can be committed by any worker in the home. Opportunities are there to take advantage of the situation and steal, commit identity theft, or even abuse the elder. Home workers may be totally unsupervised when there is no agency involved. Individual workers not screened by agencies may be uninsured and unbonded, so you have no way to recover from a theft of money or property by an independent worker. An agency should carry insurance and be bonded to protect you against loss from theft.

4. You would need to report the worker's earnings and to withhold taxes for any employee you hire.

According to the Internal Revenue Service, anyone who employs a private person on a regular basis at home has an employee, rather than an independent contractor. Accordingly, you, the employer, must withhold taxes according to the law, pay payroll tax, and report the earnings of your worker.

5. You may have to provide workers' compensation insurance.

If you hire a home worker, set the home worker's hours, and require that they work on specific days, technically, the home worker is your employee. The rules vary from state to state with regard to what workers' compensation insurance you must purchase, but, in some states, it is necessary for any employee to have workers' compensation insurance as a matter of law. The workers' compensation insurance premium may be something you did not plan on paying. It may be a requirement of your state's law that you have it, because workers can be injured on the job with lifting, carrying, and doing some of the many other things which elders require. Back injuries among caregivers are fairly common.

You could be liable for all medical costs for such an injury if your home care worker, hired independently, does not have insurance to cover medical expenses in the event of injury on the job.

6. Unemployment insurance and state disability insurance may also be a state requirement for any employee, even a part-time employee.

Check with your local and state laws to determine if you must purchase unemployment insurance for any worker, even a part-time worker, who is employed in the home. If the worker gets fired, the worker can then collect unemployment insurance until he or she has found a replacement job. Your state's employment development department may list your state's requirements on its website. Check there for the legal requirements of being an employer full time or part time.

7. The need to personally check the worker's driving record.

It will be necessary for you to check the driving record of any person whom you wish to either drive your elder's vehicle or who will transport your elder in his own vehicle.

You will need to determine whether the worker's license is valid in your state. States require some form of liability insurance on the automobile that will be driven. It will be necessary for you to determine if the liability insurance policy covering either or both vehicles you expect the worker to drive is current and adequate for the vehicle and for any person injured while driving it.

Again, this can take time. An agency, which screens its workers (as a qualified agency should do), will have workers ready to go when you call. The check for proper driver's license and insurance will already be done.

8. Independent workers may lack stability.

If you are hiring on your own, it is necessary to contemplate the possibility that the worker will suddenly quit and leave your elder without help. Workers may have to leave if a family member becomes ill or dies. The worker may get sick and be unable to work. Since one cannot necessarily anticipate such a situation in advance, you may hear without any notice that your worker has suddenly departed for another location, and you are left without any knowledge of when or if that person will return. You, as a responsible relative, can suddenly get stuck caring for your elder who has no help at home. This can interfere with your job, family, and your own responsibilities.

It is extremely difficult to find help on your own to replace a worker who departs suddenly if your elder needs help each day. The process of background checking,

checking references, and the like cannot be done instantly. An agency will work to provide you with another worker as fast as they possibly can in order to keep you as a customer.

9. Independent workers may be unreliable in assisting with medications.

Elders often have trouble keeping track of medications, keeping their prescriptions filled, and remembering when to take the medications which are prescribed for them. If an agency is involved, the agency representative or care manager can set up a system to ensure that the elder is reminded to take medicines at the proper time and in the proper amount. The agency representative can be sure that there are proper refills when the elder has run out of medication.

10. It may be more difficult to get a report of desired information.

If you live at some distance and cannot be there on a daily basis, it is much more difficult to ensure that the home worker that you hired on your own will report things to you as you wish them to be reported.

Based on the advantages and disadvantages of hiring independently, I typically recommend using an agency to find home care workers.

WHAT CAN I EXPECT FROM AN AGENCY?

An agency may cost you more than you might spend trying to hire on your own, but the extra money you will need to pay an agency to find you a qualified worker is well worth it. Quality agencies are in the business of providing competent home workers. Most of the time, the home worker provides companionship services, such as transporting the client to appointments, assistance with shopping and errands, reading and assistance with correspondence, purchasing of groceries, cooking and providing meals, and doing light housekeeping. The companionship services may also include reminding the elder to take medications at specific times throughout the day. For an elder with memory problems, you should not chance hiring an incompetent worker.

In addition, an agency will provide hands-on caregiving services, such as bathing, dressing, washing hair, grooming nails, transferring (from bed to chair, chair to bath, and back to bed), help with walking, and help with exercise programs. This is not what Medicare refers to as "skilled nursing." These very basic caregiving services are not provided by people who are licensed nurses or have nursing training in a formal program. They are considered unskilled or "custodial" services. Medicare does not pay for custodial services. If your elder needs a variety of custodial services, an agency will know the person best suited to meet your elder's needs.

Home care agencies will often provide overnight shifts if elders cannot be alone at night. Most agencies will also supply workers providing the elder with care, twenty-four hours a day. If you are attempting to hire on your own, it may be very difficult to safely find workers to cover twenty-four-hour care.

What you cannot expect from any agency is perfection. Even workers who are carefully screened do not always meet their employer's expectations, as in any employment situation. You are responsible to make sure that your elder is safe, well cared for, and that the agency is doing its job. If you are not satisfied with what the agency has provided, it is appropriate to express your dissatisfaction and ask for another worker. It is necessary to involve your aging loved one in the process when possible, since change can be much harder for elders than for more adaptable, younger people. Never change workers without asking your elder about it, making respectful suggestions, preparing your elder, and trying to get the elder to agree to the change. If your aging loved one has dementia and does not remember one day to the next, it is best to give only the information needed at the moment ("This is Jane, your helper today.") rather than burden her unnecessarily with explanations that are lost on a person who cannot process them.

DO ALL AGENCIES EMPLOY THEIR CAREGIVERS?

All agencies should thoroughly screen, background check, insure, and bond every worker they provide for you, but not all home care agencies are the employers of the workers they place with you. Agencies which serve as employers for their own workers assume responsibility for payroll, taxes, insurance, invoicing your aging parent or you, and receiving payment—including checks, credit cards, or long-term care insurance which covers such services. Generally, assessment by an agency representative is provided without additional charge.

Non-employer agencies, which function as placement agencies only, do not typically provide supervision of their workers, though some placement agencies may offer limited supervision. Ongoing supervision of workers is one of the most valuable services an employer agency—as opposed to a placement agency—can give. The agency serves as your eyes and ears. It takes responsibility for the management of the worker as well as placement.

A placement agency finds a worker, but the responsibility for what the worker does is your job to monitor. They will also screen and conduct background checks on their workers, but once the employee is placed, their role ends. The employer–employee relationship is between the aging loved one, their adult child, and the worker. The person responsible for the elder's money pays the workers directly, keeps track of invoices, and provides either a federally required W-4 tax form or a 1099 tax form for independent contractors at the year's end. Placement agencies generally do not assume the employer role because there is less risk of liability, and there are fewer complications to the job of providing caregivers if the caregivers are not the agency's employees. Agencies which act as employers of the caregiver have more risk and responsibility and more expenses than a placement-only agency.

WHO WOULD FIND OUT IF I HIRE A WORKER AND DON'T TAKE OUT TAXES?

If you are hiring a worker to take care of the elder in the elder's home, you set the hours and terms of work, and the worker is visiting regularly to do the job, the Internal Revenue Service considers the worker to be an employee, not an independent contractor. It is not likely that the IRS will come knocking on your door independently. It is certainly true that many people get away with hiring workers in the home and never paying withholding taxes (as required by the IRS), never paying workers' compensation insurance, and never paying state disability or unemployment insurance.

However, all it takes is one disgruntled former employee to contact any one of these agencies, and you risk substantial fines for failing to comply with the law. The fines can be thousands of dollars, which the IRS assesses as penalties for failure to pay the employee properly and to pay taxes as the law requires.

Likewise, your state may require you to pay workers' compensation insurance to any full- or part-time employee. If you decide to risk it and not do so, and your worker is injured and makes a claim for workers' compensation benefits, it will then quickly become known that you have failed to provide this insurance. You can become personally liable for the cost of the worker's medical treatment, no matter how long it takes.

In addition, your state may impose a fine on you if you terminate your worker and he or she does not have the opportunity to collect unemployment insurance or disability benefits. If your elder has the means to provide home help, or you do, this is not an area to scrimp. The elder's health and safety are at stake.

For further information concerning the responsible use of a quality home care agency, contact the National Private Duty Association. This is the first association for providers of private duty home care in the United States. Visit their website at PrivateDutyHomecare.org or call (317) 663-3637.

ARE HOME CARE AGENCIES LICENSED?

Home care agencies are not required to obtain an agency license in every state. Some states require only a business license for anyone to provide non-medical home care services in an individual's home. Twenty-three of our fifty states have standards requiring home care organizations to register or obtain a license. Because the requirements are different throughout the states, you as a consumer will need to determine if licenses are required in your state and whether any agency you are considering using has the required license.

Be sure to distinguish between an ordinary business license, which anyone can get to open any kind of business, and a home care license. If licenses are required in your state, there is a greater measure of security that a licensed agency will thoroughly screen and train its workers. Although even licensed agencies can end up with a bad apple of a worker, at least the screening process they normally use will improve your chances of avoiding someone with a criminal record, drug problem, poor work history, or poor suitability for the job.

THE ESSENTIAL NEED FOR A THOROUGH BACKGROUND CHECK

As technology has developed, we have the means to check out anyone we hire to do anything. Sometimes, it just doesn't occur to a person who wants to hire a home care worker that being too trusting can be a costly mistake. For elders who may be more trusting than their adult children, a smiling face, friendly manner, and pleasant conversation may be enough to cause them to trust a person who applies for a home care position. Many a con artist or thief with a pleasant demeanor has the ability to fool an elder.

I encourage every person who wishes to bring a worker into the home to get thorough information—to do a criminal background check as well as a job history background check. An all-state background check will enable you to find out if a person has committed any crimes in any other states. It will also tell you if the person has lost any state licenses or if the worker has ever filed for bankruptcy. All of these items usually show up in a background check, though the public records are not perfect. They are the best you can do. The cost of getting a background check is about one hundred dollars, according to a colleague, former criminal defense attorney Lester Rosen, author of *The Safe Hiring Manual*. His company has done reference and background checking for businesses for decades. He advises any employer to spend what it takes to do your own background check.

Agencies should be doing this kind of background check. However, since their profit margin may not be great, they do not want to spend money that they don't have before they hire someone. Some do a less expensive, in-state version only. The problem is that a convicted person can move to another state, and their past crimes can be invisible to you if you don't look further. If you aren't sure what an agency is doing to check its workers' backgrounds, please ask a lot of detailed questions about it. Essentially, you need to find out if the agency did an all-state criminal and civil background investigation.

Besides doing the background check, look the person up on the Internet. What's on their Facebook page if they have one? Are they part of any group that raises questions for you? Do your own basic search for the information the prospect has posted or that is otherwise publicly available, just as any prospective employer would.

SUMMARY

Your elder is at risk for financial and other abuse simply because of age, and particularly because of dementia and other conditions which affect mental ability.

Many home care workers are kind, dedicated people who enjoy taking care of elders. They enable your loved one to stay at home, where most elders prefer to be, and to manage the activities of daily living safely. However, not all are honest. A home setting is unsupervised, and it can be very tempting for a dishonest person to take advantage of the aging person receiving care. The message is simply: beware, and if home help is needed, get it the smart way.

Use an agency if you can, since the best agencies offer supervision of the worker. That supervision may not be something you can do yourself, and it is certainly worth the price. Even with an agency, you will still need to monitor what is going on. An employee on a relatively low salary, working in your loved one's home, unsupervised most or all of the time, may be tempted to neglect her duties, take advantage of trust, or attempt to influence your loved one to the elder's disadvantage.

By far, most home care workers are doing a fine job. However, as a family member, it is important to note that everyone you bring into a loved one's home is there with a lot of opportunity for good and bad. The more you are involved, the safer your loved one will remain.

Recommended Resources

- American Association of Retired Persons (AARP). 601 E Street NW, Washington, DC 20049. www.AARP.org.

- "In-home Care for a Loved One . . . Will You Gamble with Your Choice of Home Care?" 941 East 86th

Street, Suite 270, Indianapolis, IN 46240. www.
PrivateDutyHomeCare.org.

- "Consumer and Worker Risks from the Use of Nurse
  Registries and Independent Contractor Companies,"
  National Private Duty Association (NPDA). 941 East
  86th Street, Suite 270, Indianapolis, IN 46240. www.
  PrivateDutyHomeCare.org.

SHOULD YOUR LOVED ONE GO INTO ASSISTED LIVING?

D oes your aging loved one need help? Should your mother go to an assisted living community? Is your father better off at home?

These are some of the most frequently asked questions adult children have about their aging loved ones. In order to help with the decision making about a move from home, it is necessary to understand the fundamentals of assisted living. You'll need to know what it is, how much it costs, how to pay for it, and what it can and can't do for your loved one.

Because there is no single definition of what we sometimes call "assisted living," there is considerable confusion.

Generally, the term refers to a place where aging parents live in a group setting, often with private apartments or rooms, and where they receive assistance with personal care and meals. The confusion stems from the use of the word "care" by assisted living facilities. For the average consumer, there is an assumption about what care is when it comes to Mom or Dad. Many facilities are great places to live, since they provide many social benefits for elders who need some care but want to retain independence. There is a blurred line in many consumers' minds about the differences between assisted living facilities and nursing homes, which provide nursing care.

We hope to clear up any confusion with assisted living, some of which is created by the facility's marketing efforts, designed to get elders in, paying the fees to join the community as well as paying the monthly rent.

Please consider this chapter an introduction to understanding the differences between assisted living and skilled nursing facilities. It is not a comprehensive study of every kind of assisted living in every state. Things may be different where you live. But no matter where you are, your aging parents will get the most for their money (or yours, if you're paying) if you know what you are buying and what the limitations are with assisted living facilities. I am an advocate for allowing as much independence for elders as possible. I am also an advocate for making safe choices for aging loved ones. I hope this chapter sheds some light on a broad and perhaps confusing subject.

WHAT IS ASSISTED LIVING?

There are no uniform definitions of what this term means, and the term "assisted living" is used differently in different states. Generally, assisted living refers to facilities in which elders are housed in a communal setting with services. For purposes of this chapter, assisted living facilities will be referred to as ALFs. In some states and locations, they are also called residential care for elders (RCFEs), congregate living facilities, continuing care retirement communities, personal care homes, retirement homes, or community residences.

ALFs provide a place for elders to live independently in community settings with some personal care available. Most provide all meals, social activities and services, transportation, and assistance managing the "activities of daily living," which means walking, bathing, eating, dressing, toileting, and getting up and down from bed and chair.

Typically, an assisted living facility is regulated and licensed by the state and is built on a social model for living, rather than a medical model. What this means is that assisted living is not a medical facility with skilled nursing care available and doctors on call for its residents. Rather, it is a community setting supervised, at least theoretically, by a trained staff that assists as needed with the "custodial," rather than medical, needs of its residents. Medicare generally refers to "custodial care" as care with such things as activities of daily living which do not require skilled nursing. The terminology can be somewhat confusing to the consumer. "Long-term care" is one way in which the Assisted Living Federation of America, the assisted living industry's national organization, refers to assisted living.

However, the specifics of what "care" is allowed and expected in a non-medical setting may not be clearly explained by the industry. For the consumer, the focus of assisted living should start with a desire to meet the elder's social needs in a communal setting. Independence is emphasized more than care. With the benefit of supportive services added, an elder without complex medical care can remain relatively independent. If the elder has more complex medical needs than can be met by custodial caregivers, a skilled nursing facility (often called a nursing home) might be a better choice. Some ALFs do provide a great deal of care, however, and the line between what a skilled nursing facility can do and what an ALF can do is somewhat blurred.

WHO DECIDES WHETHER A PERSON CAN STAY IN ASSISTED LIVING?

Some ALFs have a separate skilled nursing unit or section on site. It must have a separate license to provide skilled care by licensed nurses. A resident whose medical problems increase would have to move out of the independent or assisted living portion of the facility and into its skilled nursing section when skilled nursing becomes essential. In those situations, it is usually the facility director or administration which makes the decision for the elder about when it is time to give up independent or assisted living for a skilled-care arrangement.

In some states, the issue has been disputed and courts have had to decide whether to move a resident out of the assisted living apartment and into the skilled nursing section or out of the community where no skilled nursing unit is available onsite. When courts have ruled on this question, they have given the ALF administration the right to make the decision about where the aging person must go, even over the elder's objections, and even when the elder is willing to pay out-of-pocket for extra help.

It is useful in considering assisted living to understand that even if you pay a high entrance fee, also called a "community fee," to become a resident of an independent or assisted living apartment, this does not automatically guarantee control over how long your loved one can stay there. The facility may have a right to decide when it's time to go. That kind of decision would be based on the declining state of health of a resident, such that he develops a need for a higher level of care than the community can provide.

Types of Assisted Living Facilities Include the Following:

- **Board and care.** Usually, this is a room in a private home or other building. Rooms are often shared. Meals are offered in a common dining area. Bathrooms are usually shared also. The advantage of this model is that it costs less than a private apartment, and there may be more one-on-one attention to the individual resident in a close setting. Residents do not have the option of preparing their own meals. In California, at least, the license for such a facility is through the State Department of Social Services, which is the same as for any size of assisted living facility.

- **Apartment-style with hotel-type services.** This type of setting offers independence, though meals may be offered in common dining areas. Laundry services, some social services, assistance with medications, and limited personal care may be offered.

- **Apartment-style with personal care services.** This style of ALF may have a more comprehensive array of assistance with activities of daily living and may accept incontinent residents, persons in wheelchairs, and every kind of assistance short of skilled nursing. It will likely also offer meals in a common dining area and may give residents the choice of preparing meals for themselves in their own kitchens in their apartments. Social activities, transportation to events and doctors' appointments, and supervision of general health and wellness are often provided as well.

- **Dementia care.** Some ALFs provide specific units for persons who require dementia assistance. These facilities must be specially licensed in some states. The state may require a higher ratio of staff to residents, specialized staff training to deal with dementia residents, and safety precautions to prevent confused residents from wandering outside. The kinds of apartments or private rooms available will vary from facility to facility. Ideally, such a facility will have programs for memory care, secured exits, alarm systems to notify staff of resident whereabouts, and other visual cues to help residents with memory difficulty.

Technology has advanced to the point that 24/7 electronic monitoring of residents in dementia (or other) units is available. It may be expensive to employ it, but this monitoring can allow staff to determine where a resident is at all times and to prevent confused residents from getting into dangerous situations. Personal tracking devices can be used, including GPS-enabled footwear, bracelets, and pendants, as well as movement sensors in walls and floors. All of these can improve the ability of the ALF to prevent residents from wandering outside, falling, and experiencing other mishaps. However, the technology is only as good as the staff that monitors it.

Various combinations and versions of the above kinds of living communities are available in different areas. Generally, the more services offered and the nicer looking the grounds and rooms are, the more expensive the facility is going to be.

HOW IS ASSISTED LIVING DIFFERENT FROM A NURSING HOME?

ALFs typically strive for a home-like atmosphere and work to avoid the hospital-like feel. A primary goal is to provide an enriched social setting where people can live with some basic services available on a daily basis, or as needed.

A nursing home, on the other hand, is licensed by the state's department of health and certified by Medicare and Medicaid to deliver health care. Ideally, it also offers social programs, but with licensed nursing staff onsite at all times. It must meet basic licensing and certification criteria, which federal and state regulatory agencies establish in order to be reimbursed for the daily, per resident dollar rate they seek as well as for treatments it provides.

Examples of treatments may include administration of injections, medication, assessment, wound care, administration of oxygen, and delivery of various kinds of therapy.

ALFs, unlike nursing homes, are not medical facilities and do not provide skilled care unless they do so in a separately licensed unit staffed with nurses.

ALFs may employ a nurse to generally monitor its residents, but they cannot give nursing care in such residences. They can offer advice and check temperature, pulse, respiratory rate, and blood pressure, but they are not required to do so. They are actually prohibited by law from delivering nursing care, even in emergencies. They must call 9-1-1, with few exceptions. If your aging loved one is in fragile health and you are expecting the ALF to provide close monitoring of a medical condition, you have an unrealistic expectation of what an ALF can do.

Generally, the residents of skilled nursing facilities are sicker and have more complex medical needs that require the close attention and hands-on help of nurses. For example, a person with a feeding tube into her stomach would not have access to a licensed nurse at assisted living and would need to be in a skilled-care facility. Alternatively, she would have to have an arrangement with a home health service that could provide nurses to address the maintenance and care of the feeding tube issues. That nursing care could be delivered at an assisted living facility.

Margaret's Situation

Margaret, age eighty-six, has been in assisted living for five years. She likes the environment and has friends there. She needs help with bathing, and she uses a wheelchair. She has a heart condition and needs to have her heart and blood pressure monitored closely and often. It has become more unstable lately. She does not want to move to a nursing home, though assessment of her heart condition is considered skilled care, rather than custodial care.

Margaret's doctor arranged for a home health service RN to come to her apartment to visit her once a week for monitoring of her cardiac condition and to communicate with him about necessary adjustments in her medications. Margaret is able to stay in assisted living, for now, with the help of skilled nurses from outside the facility. If her condition gets worse, the weekly visits might not be enough. If she needs oxygen, for example, it would become necessary for her to move to a skilled nursing facility or get skilled care elsewhere in a hospital or at a home with skilled nursing visits.

WHO PAYS FOR ASSISTED LIVING?

Assisted living facilities cannot bill Medicare or Medicaid for their services, since they are not health care facilities. Custodial care services are not covered by Medicare, regardless of the setting in which they are delivered. Both Medicare and Medicaid distinguish between care that is classified as custodial and that which is classified as skilled care. Therefore, most residents pay out-of-pocket for assisted living.

There are some exceptions under relatively new, experimental programs called Assisted Living Waiver Programs. These are designed to keep vulnerable residents out of nursing homes by allowing low-income residents to pay for assisted living with their existing resources, such as Social Security income. The rules are established to enable those who can't otherwise afford an assisted living facility to take advantage of not being in a nursing home and to remain in the community, which specifically means in assisted living or board and care homes. For these low-income elders, the only option other than a waiver program placement is being forced to go to nursing homes just to get some basic skilled care from nurses. Low-income individuals may also be forced to go to nursing homes because they cannot manage on their own any longer and because Medicaid will pay for long-term residency in a nursing home, while it will not do so, without a waiver program, for assisted living.

Medicaid has traditionally covered nursing home care, but not any other kind of long-term care facility. It is costly to tax payers, since nursing homes are much more expensive than most other kinds of long-term care living situations available. The waiver programs are an attempt to prevent some elders who do not need full-time nursing care from having to be in full-time nursing care facilities. The facilities are reimbursed, or subsidized, through special funding which makes up some of the difference between the resident's Social Security or Disability income and the actual cost of living in the facility. The resident pays her income to the facility, and the facility receives additional payment for care from the government-sponsored fund.

The problem is that many owners of these homes do not want to participate in these programs. Therefore, the number of choices available to a prospective resident is limited. In my area, for example, a low-income, eligible resident applied for the program, which is technically open in her county, but there are no participating homes, neither board and care nor assisted living. Her only income is Social Security, which is not enough on its own to pay for any regular board and care home. Her daughter had to take her in, or she would have had to remain in the nursing home, even though she required only minimal nursing help with her medications. She is otherwise able to care for herself with a little custodial assistance.

These waiver programs are not available in every county, nor in every state. They seem to be working well enough to have expanded recently, as of the time of this writing. There are complex requirements involved, including the rule that a person must be in a skilled nursing home to start with and must then transfer out to an ALF or board and care home that is on a list of participating facilities for the program.

We have not yet observed that the high-end, chain assisted living homes participate in the Assisted Living Waiver Programs. There is a greater likelihood that the eligible, low-income elder that needs the program will have limited choices within the program, and the available residences will be smaller and have fewer amenities.

Nine out of ten residents in ALFs pay privately. Historically and before waiver programs came into being, only those with thousands of dollars of income or disposable assets could afford assisted living. Though this is changing, payment still comes primarily from the resident and not from any program. Some aging people sell their homes to pay for assisted living. Some long-term care insurance policies also pay for all or part of the cost of assisted living.

Veteran's benefits, in the form of Aid and Attendance may, for eligible vets, pay part of the cost of being in assisted living. This benefit pays the eligible vet a set amount monthly, and it can be used to cover the monthly cost of the facility. However, in most places, the elder will also have to come up with additional money out-of-pocket to meet the full expense of an ALF.

Of special note: All information about VA benefits is available on the government's website. Under federal law, no one is allowed to charge you or your loved one to obtain information about eligibility or how to get Aid and Attendance or any other veterans' benefit. Further details about this program are discussed in Chapter Five.

Hidden Costs

The state's department of social services does not place limits on what a facility can charge its residents. The costs may vary considerably from state to state and county to county within the same state. There are numerous cost factors to consider when determining whether an elder wants to move to assisted living.

Base rent is a fixed charge, and the marketing person will tell you that when you inquire about any facility. It may sound reasonable. In California, one of the more expensive places in the United States to live, the low-end, base rent for a room or apartment may be $4000–$6000, and it can climb quite high in the nicest, best furnished ALF with the most programs and amenities.

The less obvious cost is something that most larger ALFs call "care points." This is a method devised by the industry to assign dollar charges to each increment of service offered. For instance, if the aging person needs help with bathing, there are care points assigned each month for each bath. There are care points charged for setting up medications by the medication technician, and there are care points for help with meals, walking, and other aspects of care provided by facility staff.

The more care a resident requires, the more it costs to be in an ALF, unless the person is on a special waiver program. We have known elders who are paying as much as $12,000–$16,000 a month for assisted living when a lot of custodial services are needed. In those instances, the cost of assisted living rivals or exceeds the typically much higher cost of paying out-of-pocket for skilled nursing facilities, and the ALF resident is still without skilled nursing care.

Besides the base rent and care points, the larger assisted living communities may have a separate fee to move in and become a resident. These vary widely and can be very expensive. It is not a typical first and last month's rent as one would find in an outside apartment. It can be much higher. In smaller homes, there may be no community fee at all. If you and your loved one do not turn out to like the facility, be aware that sometimes the community fee is not refundable. Be sure to read the facility's contract to learn if the fee is refundable or not.

HOW DO I DECIDE BETWEEN AN ASSISTED LIVING FACILITY AND A SKILLED NURSING FACILITY?

Where an elder should move when living at home is no longer appropriate or safe is a serious decision. One should weigh the decision very carefully, since moving an elder from place to place can be very hard on the aging person.

Confusion, getting used to a new routine, new sights and smells, different food, and new people in the environment are all factors to which the aging person must adjust.

The ability to adapt to something new may decrease with age, as most of us know. Therefore, it is important to look ahead at the elder's needs a few months or a year or two down the road, rather than simply figure out what the elder needs right now. For an aging person in a physically declining state, an ALF which also has a skilled nursing wing on site may be the best choice. You should seek medical advice about this from a physician who knows the elder.

If the aging loved one has unstable diabetes, for example, and uses insulin every day, an assisted living facility may not be able to meet his needs for increased insulin throughout the day; assisted living has no skilled nursing available to assess the changes in such a condition throughout each day, nor to adjust the insulin dosage. Any complex, changing medical condition which requires skilled nursing assessment and action, day or night, may make assisted living an unsuitable choice.

ALFs with sufficient staff and training, registered or otherwise licensed nursing supervision, and adequate safety measures for confused elders may be able to do many of the tasks performed in a skilled nursing facility.

If you are considering an ALF, ask about their ability to provide for your family member's needs. If your loved one is incontinent, has breathing difficulty, needs around-the-clock supervision, requires regular nursing assessment to remain safe, or has a combination of illnesses which require frequent monitoring by a skilled person, be cautious about moving him into an ALF. If you choose this kind of residence, you will need one that will offer skilled services in a separate unit when the anticipated need arises.

State laws prohibit a nurse employed in an ALF from delivering hands-on care, such as changing the dressings on a leg wound or inserting or removing tubes, for example. The nurse employed by an ALF may be limited to assessing and advising residents about their health care and training staff.

What Are the Advantages of Assisted Living Facilities?

There are many advantages to assisted living facilities which cannot be so readily met in other kinds of living arrangements. First, this model provides for an elder's social needs in a controlled setting, presumably with trained staff. It can do much to prevent or counteract social isolation, a major contributor to both mental and physical health risks. Many assisted living facilities work hard to provide a cheerful, enriched social environment with many choices for elders. The access to a director, caregivers, recreational and social activities, and transportation to doctors, as well as having the opportunity to eat meals in common dining areas, is conducive to enhanced mental wellness.

Some facilities are bright, nicely furnished, and have attractive amenities on site. Some are in settings with access to gardens, patios, or other outdoor locations in which elders can relax, congregate, or enjoy good weather. Many elders' physical needs do not rise to the level of requiring skilled nursing. Skilled nursing facilities are more likely to have a hospital-like look, feel, and even smell than an ALF. ALFs do not necessarily give one the impression of an institution. Many skilled nursing facilities do.

Advantages of Assisted Living Facilities:

- **Assisted living can be lower in cost than skilled nursing facilities.** Another advantage of an ALF is cost—usually, it is lower than that of a skilled nursing facility. However, as the above discussion shows us, the cost of a higher end ALF for an aging person with many needs is similar or greater than a nursing home. Smaller "board and care" or "personal care" homes are typically less costly than nursing homes. Fewer staff and simpler day-to-day activities cost less than a larger ALF with a great variety of amenities and choices for the elder.

- **You can maintain your independence.** One of the greatest advantages of ALFs is that they allow your elder to maintain her independence while still having access to help with activities of daily living. A caregiver's help with bathing, medication management, or transferring from wheelchair to bed can make enough of a difference that an elder can manage well for a time without having to consider a skilled care facility. Some residents are able to remain in ALFs for the remainder of their lives.

- **ALFs may work with the local hospice and provide end-of-life care,** an important aspect of planning ahead for an aging person. Some people are very satisfied and happy with the community feeling they get, the friends they make, and the fun they enjoy with activities available to them in this setting.

- **Feels like home.** A final advantage of an ALF is that it is likely to have a look and feel of home. Independent apartments or rooms are set up to allow for individuality. Some ALFs allow pets, and residents bring their beloved animals with them. Pets generally do not live in skilled nursing facilities, due to health regulations, though they are allowed to visit.

If given a choice, most elders would choose a pretty, well-appointed ALF before a nursing home. An ALF is simply more appealing for many who can manage without skilled nursing care and who can afford the cost.

Disadvantages of Assisted Living Facilities:

- **Expectations for monitoring and care may not be met.** There are various disadvantages of this kind of living arrangement. One disadvantage is that the elder's or elder's family's expectations as to what will be provided may not be clear. The family and the elder recognize that the elder needs care, but they may not fully understand or accept the extent of what is needed. Although the ALF will try to screen carefully to be sure the elder's needs and the facility's level of care match, this does not always work. Families may understate the elder's needs because they are in denial about them, the elder is in denial about them, or they have inadequate knowledge of what is truly needed to keep their loved one safe.

  The facility screens its prospective residents to be sure the resident meets its criteria and that the elder will fit in. Not everyone does well in community living. If the elder refuses to participate in all the programs and socialization opportunities offered, there is little point in paying for them.

- **There are unclear standards about what a community can do for your loved one.** Some ALFs offer dementia care, and some do not. Some ALFs allow people who need a wheelchair full time, and some do not, and so on. Some have many programs to choose from and some are much more limited. What your loved one needs should conform to the choice you make about which community is right.

Therefore, to avoid confusion, you need to do your information gathering before you start exploring options for assisted living. Find out from a combination of sources what your elder's needs are. Get a clear idea about any medical problems your aging loved one has after a thorough assessment by a medical doctor. You will need your elder's written permission to talk with her doctor about medical conditions and needs, due to federal laws protecting one's right to privacy about this information. If you accompany your aging family member to the doctor, it is likely that the doctor will discuss the elder's condition with you, since the doctor can ask the elder if it is okay to discuss these matters. If you plan to call on the telephone, it is less likely that the doctor's office, or the physician, will give out information.

If your aging loved one is competent enough to give you permission, and you need it in writing, ask the doctor's office to provide you with the form (called a "release of information") for your elder to sign.

Once you have a good idea from the doctor of what level of care your elder needs, you are ready to move forward with your checklist and questions in hand to determine which ALF might work for your elder. Good ALFs will also require that the doctor fill out forms, stating what the elder's condition is and what the elder needs from a medical point of view. This careful preparation will help you make a good match for your elder and an appropriate ALF or other facility.

- **Assisted living facilities can be expensive.** One is essentially paying for all of the social activities, entertainment, outings, transportation, and other amenities offered, as well as room and board, with the monthly charges. Care points, even at the lowest level, add significantly to the cost in a larger community, such as a chain. Further, costs can be raised with little notice. Most residents are on a yearly lease arrangement, but some are not. This leaves them vulnerable to rent increases that they cannot afford.

- **Monthly charges may rise.** Some larger corporations are buying up assisted living facilities in large numbers, with the apparent goal of becoming the largest chains in the country. This has a downside in that with a facility's new ownership, monthly charges may rise, management may change, and what was once comfortable and predictable can give way to sweeping changes the resident did not agree to upon entry.

Charlie's Facility Changes Ownership

I recently visited an assisted living facility where a relative resides. He is happy there, but had only recently moved in. During the time family was arranging for his apartment there, the facility was sold and changed its name. After just a few months, it was sold again, this time to a very large chain with a less-than-ideal reputation. Rents went up for those who did not have a lease in place before the sale. Sadly, many of them had to move out, even after years of being there because they could not afford the new, higher monthly costs on their fixed incomes.

WHAT ELSE SHOULD I KNOW ABOUT ASSISTED LIVING?

A consumer can expect the ALF to provide what it promises to provide: a sense of community, a place to live safely, and supportive services and care. ALFs typically require that the resident or resident's representative sign a contract, agreeing to the conditions of residency and for payment of the fees charged. The elder should receive what the contract says the ALF will give. Some elders or their family members become upset with facilities because the care delivered is not up to the level they expect. Others are satisfied and eventually adjust well to the environment. If you are dissatisfied, it is important to seek a meeting with the director of the facility.

Sometimes dissatisfaction arises from the expectation that a staff member will be watching over the resident twenty-four hours a day. Although supervision of residents is essential, and staff is available all day, this does not mean that a resident gets 24/7 care. Any elder who truly needs care full time probably needs a skilled nursing facility. Staff at an ALF is sparse at night, particularly.

To prevent misunderstandings and dissatisfactions, make sure you do the following things:

Ask for complete disclosure of all health-related services.

You should expect complete disclosure of all health-related services and custodial care services available, and the cost of each. You need a written breakdown of all care point charges. You should expect to learn in writing, as a part of the contract, what the terms are for termination of residency, including transfer to a hospital or nursing facility.

The elder has a right to know what happens if he has a complaint against a facility and to whom the complaint should be taken. The facility should reveal what it is licensed to do and what it is not licensed to do. Since this varies within states and between states, be sure to ask about what the facility cannot do if it is not spelled out in the contract.

Review the contract.

The contract to become a resident can be complex. If the legal language is confusing, seek advice from an attorney familiar with this field to be sure you know what you are signing. Never agree to put up your own assets as collateral for a loved one to be admitted to a facility unless you plan to use your own assets to pay for his stay there over the long run. Either your loved one can afford the facility or not.

Be a savvy consumer.

Many facilities have websites, photographs, and printed brochures; these can help you screen out which ones you do not think are suitable. A marketing director representing the ALF in a larger facility is likely to be the person showing you around. The marketing director's job is to show the facility in its best light. A good consumer will look beyond that to find out the details the marketing person may not tell you to be sure the ALF you are considering is the right fit.

Understand that price is not a guarantee of quality.

Price is a major consideration, but a high monthly cost is not a guarantee of anything. Look beyond the lovely antique furniture, fancy amenities, and extensive menus to the frequency of contact by staff with your loved one. If an elder is a bit shy, is there someone on staff who will take the time to draw her out and help her engage in things? If your elder has experienced a sense of loss, is there an empathetic staff person to talk to? Consider that your loved one could spend the rest of her life in this facility. Take the time to choose very carefully, and make the best move possible under your circumstances.

Once your elder is committed to an ALF and has moved in, it will be expensive, stressful, and even traumatic to have to make another change and start over. Do all you can to be helpful in the decision making process. The American Association of Retired Persons (AARP) provides a useful checklist on its website, AARP.org. If you are shopping for an ALF, make a copy of the checklist for each facility you are looking at and compare them after you have seen the ones you might want to choose. Look for the "Assisted Living: What to Ask" checklist for a thorough outline of questions to ask and observations to make.

HOW DO I GET MY LOVED ONE TO MOVE WHEN THE TIME COMES?

It is generally difficult to persuade an aging family member that the time has come to live in a facility, even a nice one. Of course, as with any change, it is important to talk with your elder about the possibility of change before you begin the search for an ALF. Involve him in the decision making process if he is competent to do so. Do your research and narrow the field down to a few facilities. Invite your loved one to view them with you. If his stamina is limited, check out one or two at a time.

Ask for your loved one's permission to talk about this subject. If you meet resistance, wait a while and bring it up again. Insist gently that you must do this for your peace of mind—keep bringing it up. Enlist the help of family members, if you have any, who are willing to be present and give you emotional support in the process of discussing the move.

If you are in disagreement with other family members about a move to an ALF, there are things you can do to address this problem. (See chapter two, "The Path to Peace in Family Arguments about Aging Parents," for more information.) Try empathizing with your loved one, rather than arguing with him. You can avoid argument by simply acknowledging the elder's feelings and not saying that you disagree. For example:

Elder: "I don't want to go to one of those places. I'm fine here."

Adult child: "I'm sure the thought of moving is hard for you."

Elder: "I can't do it."

Adult child: "It won't be easy. I'll help you pack up and choose what to take with you."

Elder: "You can't make me."

Adult child: "Let's not argue about this."

The transition can be easier with proper preparation, respect for your loved one, and taking your time to get her used to the idea. Many ALFs will allow you to come and share a meal there to try out the dining room. Ask to speak to a resident with whom your elder might identify, and have the ALF director or marketing person introduce him to your elder. A conversation with someone who lives in the ALF can be reassuring to your elder and to you. If you are a family member, you may wish to speak to the family member of another resident also. Ask what it is like from the family's point of view at this ALF. It is essentially a reference.

Find out if there are any complaints. If you are unsure, ask the director about how the complaints are handled. In summary, educate yourself as much as you can about any prospective ALF. Do not take the director's word for everything. They want to sell you on their facility. Be sure it is right for you from your own observations, too, beyond the sales pitch.

UNDERSTAND THAT OPERATORS OF FACILITIES ARE NOT ALL EQUAL AND THAT INCOMPETENCE EXISTS IN A FEW PLACES

The assisted living industry is far less regulated than the nursing home industry. This may make it easier for incompetent facility operators to do a poor job caring for aging loved ones in ALFs than if they were more closely watched or inspected. The best protection you have is to stay in frequent contact with your loved one there and to avoid assuming that everyone in an ALF is doing a perfect job at all times.

The most vulnerable residents are those with cognitive impairment or those who cannot communicate their own needs clearly. They need oversight, ideally from visiting family members. If you do not live nearby or cannot visit regularly, consider hiring a care manger to be your eyes and ears for checking in on your loved one regularly. How to find and use a care manager is explained in Chapter Four on distance caregiving.

Lawsuits against assisted living facilities have occurred, particularly for gross neglect of an aging, vulnerable person with dementia. Terrible harm has occurred to residents in these facilities, though these instances are rare when compared with the number of elders who are doing fine in assisted living. Family will need to be conscious of its own responsibility to watch over a loved one in assisted living from the time a family member becomes a resident to the end of the stay there.

SUMMARY

Assisted living facilities are a helpful alternative for some elders who can no longer live alone or without any help with daily activities. There are some misconceptions about them, and it is important for every family considering assisted living to understand both the pros and cons of this kind of living arrangement. Most ALFs are paid for from the elder's own resources, not from any kind of insurance. The expense of assisted living, especially if it is incurred over a period of years, may deplete all of an older person's resources. One of the most important things to remember about choosing an assisted living facility is to be a good consumer. Learn all the details and costs of the facility under consideration and ask a lot of questions. Do not assume that they will care for a loved one who needs skilled nursing in an assisted living facility. No nursing is provided. Rather, these facilities offer an enriched social environment with basic help for a person who may have trouble with activities of daily living. They are a fine solution for some but unsuitable for others.

Recommended Resources

- American Association of Retired Persons (AARP). 601 E Street NW, Washington, DC 20049. www.AARP.org.

- National Center for Assisted Living. 1201 L Street, N.W., Washington, DC 20005. www.AHCAncal.org.

HOW TO CHOOSE A
NURSING HOME

"Promise you'll never put me in one of those places."

Have you ever heard that from an aging parent? Nursing homes are perceived—whether accurately or not—as places for decrepit people to go and wait to die. They have a bad stigma.

The purpose of this chapter is to help you understand what a nursing home is and is not, and how to choose the right one if you are ever faced with that decision. Many adult children and other family members will eventually have to deal with a nursing home for a loved one, whether the stay is for a few weeks or longer.

Nursing homes provide a level of skilled care that assisted living cannot provide. They also provide a kind of care and rehabilitation that hospitals do not provide, except on a very short-term basis. After hospitalization due to an illness, surgery, or other traumatic event, your loved one may be sent to a skilled nursing facility (also referred to as a SNF or nursing home), whether you agree or not. Skilled nursing facilities must accept persons with advanced needs for care, such as feeding tubes, IVs, oxygen, infections, and chronic, progressive disease, etc. Therefore, they must have the equipment, hospital beds, nursing staff, and physician presence to do the job. The level of skilled care provided will preclude many attractive amenities one would find in an independent living arrangement.

My message is simple: Be a good consumer if you need to place your aging parent or loved one in a skilled nursing facility. Be vigilant—you can find out which are the better nursing homes and which are not good by doing your research. You will be better off if you take your time to do your research in advance, rather than waiting until a disaster happens and then having two days' notice to move your loved one to a nursing home. I hope this chapter will help you make the best choice you can for your loved one.

There are, in fact, so many tools and resources available to help you find a nursing home that it is easy to get overwhelmed with the amount of information. This chapter is an effort to help you navigate your way through the maze of sites and tools so that you can go about your search for a nursing home for your aging parent in a logical and systematic way whenever possible. I have reviewed several Internet sites with guides built into them, and I point out the strengths and weaknesses I see in of each of them.

I also have a great deal of personal experience with nursing homes that dates from my teenage years when I volunteered as a candy striper (we wore striped aprons) in a nursing home. Not only did I work in them as an aide when studying nursing, but I also worked part-time jobs in them as an RN after I received my license. Later, as a public health nurse, I had the responsibility to visit patients in the worst nursing homes, checking on elders who had previously been neglected there.

As a lawyer, I have filed lawsuits against a few nursing homes for neglect of my clients. I have also personally placed a loved one in a nursing home and helped my nearby family members do the in-person check of the choices available, since I lived at a distance from where the placement needed to be. At the end of this chapter, I share the checklist I developed for placing an elder in an appropriate SNF.

WHY WOULD MY LOVED ONE HAVE TO GO TO A NURSING HOME?

We may promise that we will never put a parent in a nursing home, thinking that nursing homes must be terrible. We may never think far enough ahead to foresee that when our aging parents live longer than we thought they might, they have more health risks. We may never consider that if a parent has a stroke or falls and breaks a hip, they will likely go to a hospital and then be sent to a nursing home for rehabilitation. A nursing home is also called a rehab facility, a convalescent home, a long-term care facility, part of a Residential Care for Elders Facility (RCEF), or other names. These various designations generally mean that the facility has licensed nurses and, usually, that it provides other skilled services, such as physical therapy, occupational therapy, and speech therapy.

Medicare pays for hospital care for most of our loved ones who are sixty-five years of age and who have applied for Medicare and are eligible to receive it. But Medicare is not an unlimited kind of insurance. The number of days compensated for in an acute care hospital is limited, and our loved one's condition will dictate how long the doctors there can treat her and expect to be paid by Medicare. If she gets better and needs less physician monitoring, the case manager is obligated to review the situation and make recommendations to discharge her from the hospital. Assuming that your loved one still needs certain kinds of skilled care, she will be transferred to a nursing home or sent home. This process can take place on short notice. How far in advance you will know about it depends on various factors, such as the efficiency of the hospital's case manager to work with doctors to recommend discharge and how stable your loved one's medical condition is.

WHO GOES TO NURSING HOMES AND WHO LIVES IN NURSING HOMES?

People go to nursing homes for shorter-term stays to recover from surgeries, to use the rehabilitation services available there, and to see how much progress they can make within the time period that Medicare will cover services in a skilled nursing facility. The maximum allowed under Medicare is one hundred days, and that is broken down into segments. Generally, nursing homes provide shorter-term services over a period of a few weeks to three months or so, and your loved one will either have to pay out of pocket after that or go to a different kind of nursing home.

Although I covered this in chapter five, I will review the difference between Medicare and Medicaid. This difference is important to understand if your aging loved one has a low income or few assets.

Medicare is a federal program of health insurance. It was created primarily for those aged sixty-five and older. One must apply to receive it, since it is not automatic. When one becomes eligible for Social Security and accepts it, the person also usually applies to receive Medicare. Medicare is divided into four major parts: The hospitalization, or Part A, and the outpatient division, Part B. Part C applies to Medicare Advantage plans, which are not discussed in this book. There is yet another part, which is the outpatient prescription drug coverage, or Part D. I simplify the explanation here, only to help you understand nursing homes. All the essential details about Medicare are available on Medicare.gov, the government's official site, which explains eligibility, costs, application, and that Medicare only pays 80 percent of covered services.

Medicaid, on the other hand, does not have an age requirement. It is financed by a combination of federal, state, and local county funds. Medicaid is specifically designed to insure low-income individuals and their families who qualify. It has many restrictions which vary from state to state. However, one thing all states have in common is that a low-income person with limited assets can qualify for Medicaid, and it will pay for a long-term stay in a nursing home. It does not pay for assisted living, generally. The few exceptions are in specific programs in some states and in certain designated counties. Those are the Assisted Living Waiver Programs, which we discussed in the previous chapter.

Medicare will pay only for a short-term stay in a nursing home, covering a staggered decreasing percentage of the stay, for as long as the nursing home patient qualifies, up to a maximum of one hundred days.

If a person qualifies for Medicaid in addition to Medicare (called a "dual eligible"), when Medicare stops paying and the person still needs to stay in a SNF, Medicaid will take over paying the bill for the resident's stay. If a person is not eligible for Medicaid because they have too much money in the bank or their income is above the Medicaid limit, they must pay out of pocket for their continued stay in a nursing home. Even if a person who has only Medicare (not a dual eligible) still needs long-term skilled nursing care beyond the hundred-day limit,, Medicare stops paying.

Not all nursing homes accept Medicaid. Not all nursing homes accept long-term residents who must stay there for lack of any alternative as low-income, Medicaid recipients. When a person qualifies for long-term care—due to physical needs—and is eligible for Medicaid, Medicaid will pay for the cost of their stay.

Almost half of the people who live in nursing homes are age eighty-five or older. Three-fourths of those in nursing homes need help with activities of daily living—such as bathing, feeding, dressing, toileting, walking, and transferring from bed to chair. More than half of nursing home residents are incontinent of bowel or bladder. Dementia is one of the most common reasons a person needs to live in a nursing home. People live in nursing homes because their physical or mental condition warrants it, or because they have become impoverished by the cost of care at home or elsewhere, and they cannot meet their needs outside a nursing home. Another important factor which causes some people to move into nursing homes is social isolation and lack of family or other support. The government refers to those in nursing homes as our "frail elderly."

WHERE DO I GO TO GET INFORMATION ABOUT NURSING HOMES IN MY AREA?

Fortunately, there are many resources available to give you objective information to guide you. First, allow yourself to stop feeling guilty. Generally it takes an entire team of people, from administrators to dietary workers, therapists, nurses, and nurse's aides, to manage infirm, incontinent, dependent, and frail elders. If you and your family are not able to take on the burden that a team of people in a facility would normally bear, there may not be a choice about whether to place your elder loved one in a facility. You will probably feel better about this difficult decision if you prepare yourself for the transition by getting the best information available.

Do your research. There is data available from agencies such as your area Agency on Aging and on the Internet. A general Internet search is likely to lead to over a dozen sites from official-sounding organizations. Our review of popular websites on how to choose a nursing home is summarized here with some tips on where to start and how to use the published information. These organizations have websites as well as toll-free numbers to help you get answers to most questions.

American Association of Retired Persons (AARP): AARP.org

Start with consumer-oriented website information. Performance data—rather than advertising—is a smart place to search. Consumer-friendly organizations such as the American Association of Retired Persons (AARP) and Consumer Reports offer good guidelines. The AARP website publishes a state-by-state guide to 17,000 Medicare and Medicaid-certified nursing home facilities. You can search by your state, county, and city. The guide also refers you to local resources in each state, which may publish a "report card" for each facility. Some states provide information about the state's health department inspections, whether citations were issued for violations, and information about complaints.

Click on the section, "Long-Term Care," which is under the home page of the AARP website, and go to "Guide to Long-Term Care." There is a brief section entitled "Starting the Nursing Home Search," which is also helpful. There is a Nursing Home Checklist, but it falls short of giving enough detail on how to research a facility for special needs, such as Alzheimer's patients. Other sites have better checklists, as discussed below.

Consumer Reports: ConsumerReports.org

Consumer Reports provides state-by-state information on quality, well-run nursing homes, as well as homes you may want to avoid. Nursing homes are required to comply with federal and state laws to receive Medicare and Medicaid reimbursement for their services. Both the federal and state governments must inspect homes regularly to see that they are in compliance with the law. This site provides information about which homes were fined for being out of compliance. Fines for violations are a warning sign to the consumer. You should check out the history of any home you are considering to be sure it does not have a history of getting fines for poor care or other violations of the law. The information is on the website, via the Nursing Home Quality Monitor. The services are free, though you may need to enroll online as a subscriber.

The Quality Monitor ranks all nursing homes in a state according to scores received for standard quality of care measures in each home, taking particular note of deficiencies that would put a resident in immediate jeopardy or cause actual harm. Those homes that failed to make routine state inspection survey results available to residents and their families are noted. The Consumer Reports section reviews the three most recent survey results for a home to determine how well they are complying with federal regulations. Homes are ranked according to their aggregate deficiency score. Homes that scored in the top 10 percent are rated as potentially good homes; those in the bottom 10 percent are the worst performers. Do not choose a nursing home without knowing what deficiencies have been found there.

According to Consumer Reports, not-for-profit nursing homes are more likely to provide good care than for-profit homes. This is based on their analysis of state inspection surveys, staffing, and quality indicators. Similarly, independently run homes are more likely to provide good care than chains.

This site also lists an Eldercare Locator number (1-800-677-1116) that can be used to reach your local Agency on Aging. This resource can supply you with a list of nursing homes and contact information for the local ombudsman, who works in counties to provide consumers with local information about care facilities.

Another useful feature of this website is the section on how to read the form which provides state survey results for each nursing home the federal government inspects in its regular survey procedures. It is called the CMS Form 2567, referring to the Centers for Medicare and Medicaid Services. The survey results are publicly available, since each licensed facility is required to publish the results.

Long-Term Care Living: LongTermLiving.org

The American Health Care Association at AHCA.org, together with the National Center for Assisted Living at AHCAncal.org, sponsors a free facility-finder service at their website, LongTermCareLiving.com. The site is comprehensive, in that it focuses on nursing homes and assisted living facilities and gives useful tips for making the transition. The site also contains helpful background information, which can be used in conjunction with a checklist. The checklist it offers is not comprehensive enough to serve the purpose of helping you choose between or among facilities, but it does provide some useful questions to ask. Use their checklist, along with others, to be sure you ask enough questions when you go to visit a facility you may be considering.

National Citizens' Coalition for Nursing Home Reform: NCCNHR.org

The National Citizens' Coalition for Nursing Home Reform is a group that dedicates itself to improving the quality of care in nursing homes by empowering consumers and citizens. It is a group comprised of consumers and advocates who need long-term care information. It has a political voice and seeks to influence public policy to improve the care of elders.

On their website, select "A Consumer Guide to Choosing a Nursing Home," which, while lengthy, is absolutely worth reading. It provides detailed background information on nursing homes, as well as information on what experts to consult in your search. It outlines the cost of homes, family involvement, staffing information, inspection reports, and the like. There are helpful tips and cautions throughout the article. These are practical reminders of what to look for in your research. One drawback to this site is that it discusses Medicare's website, Nursing Home Compare, at some length, which seems to suggest that Medicare's website is reliable. The Consumer Reports publication cautions that the Medicare website may not provide updated information, and that you should not depend on it.

Additional consumer advocacy websites include: National Consumer Voice for Quality Long-Term Care (www.HealthFinder.gov) and the National Center for Assisted Living (AHCAncal.org/ncal)

Medicare (Nursing Home Compare): Medicare.com

The official Medicare website (which is found under the US Department of Health and Human Services' main site: HHS.gov) has a search tool, Nursing Home Compare, which is intended to assist you in searching for a nursing home. It has many limitations, besides being unlikely to have the most updated information available at other sites. I find it somewhat confusing and difficult to navigate. Furthermore, it does not provide information on nursing homes that are certified at the state level. The website does give you Medicare and Medicaid certified facilities that offer skilled nursing as well as a "Resource Locator," which can guide you to other elder care websites. It has a broad range of information going far beyond finding a nursing home.

One useful part of the Medicare website is a good nursing home checklist. Again, it may be difficult to navigate the site and find this. Once you are at the Nursing

Home Compare website, navigate to the "About" section, choose "Quality Measures," and then scroll down to the "Understanding Nursing Home Quality Measures" article until you see a link entitled, "Nursing Home Checklist." Print this out and use it as one of your tools when you visit nursing homes. It can help you find the right questions to ask as you determine which nursing home will protect and support your aging loved one.

A few years ago Medicare launched a new addition to its website, called the "Ask Medicare pages." This addition may be useful to answer billing questions, figure out how to get health information for your aging parent, and get help if you are confused about coverage. It also contains information about long-term care options.

My Brother

When my brother, in his sixties, suffered a major stroke, I found myself with the responsibility of choosing a nursing home for him. He had been hospitalized for a time and had regained some of his abilities. Then he needed a lot of therapy. I was the decision maker among my other siblings because I had the necessary background in nursing.

The hospital team caring for my brother wanted to move him to a rehabilitation facility. I had to start the search for the right one. There were various choices in the area, and I was given a list, without any recommendation, by the case manager. I had visited my brother often, but lived hundreds of miles away. However, I had two siblings in the area of the hospital, so I called on them to help me.

The first place I went was California's version of the National Citizens' Coalition for Nursing Home Reform. It is called California Advocates for Nursing Home Reform (CANHR). It is an excellent consumer advocacy organization, and I knew some of the people there. The website has a list of every nursing home in the state by county. They provide publicly available data on which homes have been prosecuted by the state for violations of the applicable laws. They list how many have been found deficient by the state investigators and which have been fined. They also list, by year, the number of complaints and which homes take Medicare and Medicaid.

This information really helped narrow the search. I contacted the case manager and asked her about one in particular. She said she had gotten positive feedback about it.

I then took my own checklist for checking out a nursing home and gave it to my sister to use when she visited the facility in person. She went through the checklist, and the facility passed with flying colors. My brother had a helpful stay there until he was discharged to an assisted living facility. My checklist is at the end of this chapter.

AFTER THE BACKGROUND RESEARCH, WHAT'S NEXT?

After you do the background research and find a good home or homes to check, it is necessary to visit in person and ask questions. There is no substitute for a personal visit. Your first impressions count. If you are uncomfortable the minute you walk in the door because the administrator, marketing director, or other person you encounter seems unfriendly, pay attention. The facility attitude may reflect the care rendered there.

If you are met by a friendly person, use the checklist of your choice and ask questions about the facility and what your elder can expect. Discuss the details of care your loved one needs. If your aging parent has dementia, find out about the care for persons with this disease. If she needs help eating, ask about how many staff members are available at mealtimes to feed residents. Think through your loved one's day, and cover all parts of it. Work to find out if the facility appears able to meet the needs of your loved one, with his preferences, personality traits, and quirks.

Ask to speak with a visiting family member of someone who lives in the nursing home. Find out that person's impressions of the nursing home. Employees of the facility often talk amongst themselves. Listen in on any conversations which take place in your presence. If they are complaining, what do they complain about? Not enough staff? This is definitely a bad sign. Observe how employees of the facility react to requests for help from residents. Are they prompt? Do they ignore the call bell? Notice how long it takes for them to respond to a resident's call bell.

Notice how often the maintenance staff cleans the rooms and how well they do so. In this era of superbugs, such as Methicillin Resistant Staph Aureus (MRSA), cleaning of the rooms should be very thorough and regular. Nursing home residents are physically vulnerable to begin with, and living in close quarters increases the chances of infection. Some nursing homes take everything out of the room to clean floors and walls. Others do a more perfunctory job, going around furniture. Observe their procedure when you are checking out nursing homes. Walk the corridors and make mental notes.

DANGER SIGNS

The dangers of the worst nursing homes are too numerous to count. Published stories of terrible abuse and neglect have appeared in the media for some time. Medicare and Medicaid have lengthy regulations of every sort, but both governmental entities lack the resources to regularly inspect homes often enough to be sure that all regulations are followed and that all deficiencies found are corrected as the law requires. Further, the government does not have the resources to fight every battle the nursing homes raise over every citation.

Citations

Nursing homes that are cited for violations may appeal the citation, spend a lot of money on lawyers to try to get the degree of the citation reduced, and otherwise make efforts to hide the extent of their failures from the public. The worst homes tend to have the same violations over and over again.

When you check websites to find out the history of citations by Medicare and Medicaid (CMS), it is a danger sign if a facility is repeatedly cited for the same violations over a period of years. It is also a danger sign if you know the history of violations, inquire about the violations when you go to the facility to check it out, and you are given a vague answer or no answer to your inquiry. The administrator should be able to explain how the facility corrected any deficiencies CMS found. Avoid facilities which do not or cannot answer questions about correcting deficiencies the government found and for which they were cited in the past.

Evidence of Understaffing

When you walk the corridors, notice how many residents are alone, lined up along the walls in wheelchairs, doing nothing. If you go more than once and see long rows of residents who look as if they need attention, but there is no one around, this may also be a danger sign. Neglect is a persistent problem in nursing homes. It usually arises from the chronic problem of insufficient staffing. It takes a special person to work in a nursing home. Some of the nursing assistants and nursing staff in nursing homes are dedicated, responsible, and very caring. It is their life's work to bring good care and attention to the elderly residents there. Others have a far less interested attitude.

Criminal neglect, assault, negligence, and other sad situations result from understaffing. The facility has a very difficult job as elders may wander, may be unpredictable, and have changing needs. However, it is their obligation to provide safe and sufficient care. Be alert to what you see on your preliminary visits. We recommend more than one. Drop in unexpectedly and see how it looks when the facility is not taking you on a tour.

Find out the staff turnover rate. Unfortunately, the rate of staff changes in nursing homes is persistently high. There are many reasons for this, including nursing shortages, low rates of pay, the difficulty of the work, the sometimes uncaring attitude of the ownership (which may focus on profits more than quality of care, in some cases), and our society's attitude toward the very oldest members among us. It is a nationwide problem. The primary caregivers are the nurse's aides. They must be certified and trained. Ask about the training, and particularly about staff turnover among the nurse's aides, also called nursing assistants. If you are able to locate a facility with longevity of employees, including head nurses and administrators, that is a good sign. High staff turnover is a danger sign.

Lack of Water Pitchers

Dehydration is a very serious and dangerous problem in nursing homes, especially for residents who have trouble holding a glass or who have a poor memory and do not remember to drink water. Dehydration can lead to bladder infections, altered mental status, and poor skin tone, among other things. Those, in turn, lead to more serious complications. Find out about how often water pitchers are filled by the staff. If you do not see water pitchers in all the rooms you pass or you do not see anyone ever filling them, it is a danger sign.

Insufficient Fall Prevention Measures

Falls are an enormous problem for elders. Aging affects balance, as do limited vision, slowed reaction time, blood pressure changes, and many other physical conditions. Confusion and poor memory may lead elders to get up without help and forget directions to do or not do as they are told. The facility must anticipate this and take safe steps to address the risk of falls. Ask about the measures in place and how often they are used.

This is an important area to ask about if your aging loved one needs help with walking, yet has a tendency to forget to ask for help. Do not accept the answer, "We use a chair alarm." The chair alarm is a device designed to sound off when an elder gets up from a chair. It connects to the elder on one end and to the wheelchair or other chair at the other end. The problem with this device is that an elder can get up and fall in a second or two. Staff cannot get there fast enough for residents who are at risk for falls, if they do not happen to be standing next to the elder when he gets up and sets off the chair alarm. The chair alarm is only a solution for people who are safe on their feet but may wander. They are not a safe fall-prevention device.

Find out about the philosophy of the nursing home concerning use of restraints, particularly if your elder is dangerous on his feet. This is a controversial subject. Nursing home residents should never be unduly restrained so as to put them in danger from the restraint itself (belts, jackets, wrist ties, etc.). At the same time, keeping a wandering person safely belted into a chair, if he is always at risk for getting up and falling, may be essential to prevent worse harm. It is a question of common sense, compassion, and wise medical and nursing judgment to decide whether to restrain a wandering resident who is at great risk for falls. No facility can keep an eye on every resident at every minute of every day.

Occasionally restraints are helpful. Though they reduce an aging person's freedom of movement, that very freedom resulting in a fall and fracture can be worse than the loss of freedom of movement. The consideration of restraints should always be carefully analyzed, discussed, and decided upon by licensed and experienced staff and employed only with physician's orders.

Skin Care Concerns

Skin breakdown of an elder can occur very quickly. It leads to pressure ulcers, bedsores, or areas of open skin, often on the tailbone area, buttock, hip, or heel, which can lead to very serious complications. Skin breakdown has many causes, one of which is neglect of the facility staff to turn and move bedbound and immobilized residents often enough. Ask how the facility deals with pressure ulcers and what policies they have to prevent skin breakdown. In your review of the history of citations a nursing home may have received, beware of any which mention decubitus ulcers, which is another way of describing pressure ulcers or skin breakdown.

If you visit an elder in a nursing home, you are unlikely to see or know about a pressure sore unless you ask or check the skin yourself. People who sit in wheelchairs for hours each day are at particular risk if they cannot get up without help. The best facilities track how often each resident moves around and takes weight off the vulnerable, bony areas of the body most subject to this serious risk. A good facility will be sure your aging loved one is walked, moved, turned, or otherwise has her position changed every two hours. This is the standard for preventing skin breakdown in any kind of facility which gives nursing care to dependent people.

With all of these red flags in mind, you will be better prepared to avoid dangerous living situations. Good nursing homes do exist. Dedicated staff and a caring philosophy are possible to find.

BE YOUR LOVED ONE'S ADVOCATE

If other family members are also able to visit, aim for a location which will allow them to share the task of overseeing the safety of your loved one. If you are not in an urban area, or a suburban area with numerous nursing homes to choose from, you may not be able to decide based on the factors we discuss in this book. If you are limited to one or two facilities because that is all that is available, you simply must become the *safety police.*

Do not rest assured that the nice people in that nursing home will always do their job properly. Assume that every nursing home has some risks, that no caregivers are perfect, and that you will need to oversee everything to be sure that Mom, Dad, or Auntie is handled correctly. One of the most loving things you can do for a vulnerable elder is to protect him from lack of care or from poor care.

That means establishing a working relationship with those in charge at the nursing home from the beginning. Let the charge nurse and administrator know that you expect to be informed of any changes in your loved one's condition. Some elders have no one to visit them. It is sad to see what happens to them. I have no doubt, after working in nursing homes, that those who have attentive families who visit often get better care. It is important to be courteous and respectful to the nursing home staff, as well as to let them know that they are accountable to you. Expressing your appreciation to them for the hard work they do also helps. Once you place your elder in a nursing home, expect that you will need to watch over him for as long as he is there. Look for a facility which will accept or welcome your input. If you need information about your loved one's status, ask to participate in the care conferences which the staff conduct to review the progress of therapy and treatment. You have a right to be there as your loved one's advocate.

CONTRACTS IN NURSING HOMES

Nursing homes will likely have a contract for becoming a resident in the home, and the elder or family member in charge is required to sign it. Just as with assisted living facility contracts: never, ever agree to put up your own assets—such as your home—as collateral for allowing your loved one to be admitted to a nursing home unless you are prepared to give up your home to pay the bill if necessary. If he has low income, you need to apply immediately for Medicaid. A good facility will help with this process. If your elder has assets and does not qualify for Medicaid, he may have to spend them on the care there to become eligible for Medicaid later on. In any case, if any facility wants you, the family member, to agree in advance to pay for a nursing home stay yourself, you should politely refuse unless you are quite wealthy and choose to do so. They can't force you to put up your house or other assets for your parent.

There is a kind of law called "filial support law," which, in some states, gives a nursing home the right to go after family members for an unpaid bill of a parent from a nursing home stay. We do not go into detail here about the complexities of these laws, but you should be aware that a low-income citizen without assets will qualify for Medicaid, and it pays for nursing home care. If Medicaid is used as it is designed, no adult child should have to be sued under a filial support law to pay for an aging parent's nursing home bill.

SUMMARY

While going to a nursing home is no one's first choice, it may become necessary for your loved one at some time. There are ways to choose a good facility, and doing your research is essential. A nursing home can give good care, or it can be a dangerous place for a vulnerable elder. If you have a loved one in a nursing home, you will need to be the safety police to ensure that he receives proper care.

You can best prepare for the experience by planning ahead, visiting often, and paying attention to what care your loved one needs and receives. Watch for the danger signs, and you will have the best chance of avoiding the worst problems. Anyone in a nursing home needs an advocate. You can become a good advocate for your loved one.

Recommended Resources

- American Association of Retired Persons (AARP). 601 E Street NW, Washington, DC 20049. www.AARP.org.

- The American Geriatric Society (AGS) Foundation for Health in Aging. The Empire State Building, 350 Fifth Avenue, Suite 801, New York, New York 10118. www. HealthInAging.org.

- American Health Care Association. 1201 L Street, N.W., Washington, DC 20005. www.AHCA.org.

- Consumer Reports. 101 Truman Avenue, Yonkers, NY. 10703-1057. www.ConsumerReports.org/nursinghomes.

- Long-Term Care Living. 1201 L Street, NW, Washington, DC 20005. www.LongTermCareLiving.com.

- Medicare (Nursing Home Compare). www.Medicare.gov.

- National Citizens' Coalition for Nursing Home Reform. 1828 L Street, NW, Suite 801, Washington, DC 20036. www.NCCNHR.org.

- US Department of Health and Human Services. 200 Independence Avenue, S.W., Washington, DC 20201. www.HHS.gov.

- California Advocates for Nursing Home Reform. 650 Harrison Street, San Francisco, CA 94107 (415) 974-5171 www.CANHR.org.

PROTECTING OUR AGING PARENTS FROM

ABUSE

This chapter is written with hope. I am only one voice, but I want to bring a serious problem to light and help anyone who reads this to understand that we all bear some responsibility to protect our aging loved ones.

Abuse of aging persons in our society is not something that just happens to other people. It can happen to someone in your own family. The older your aging parent gets, the more likely she is to be abused by someone in some way.

The focus of this chapter is on financial abuse, though abuse can be physical, emotional, or verbal. It is a complex problem with many possible causes. My intention in focusing on abuse, and on financial abuse in particular, is that I want to raise awareness so that you can be on the alert, ready to take preventive action, and recognize the risks of doing nothing.

Dedicated people across our country are working hard to help increase awareness of elder abuse, educating the public about how prevalent and devastating it is. I count myself among those dedicated people and hope you can see why I am passionate about prevention.

We may not be able to stop this enormous problem, but each individual can do much to reduce the losses and to prevent abuse you see coming in your own family.

WHAT IS ELDER ABUSE?

The term is defined by senior organizations, in books, and by law. My own state, California, has a special elder abuse law that sets out why the legislature considers elders vulnerable and why such a law is needed. It defines abuse in specific terms as doing harm to an elder (a person sixty-five or older) or a dependent adult (eighteen or older) physically, emotionally, or financially. I paraphrase here, to keep it simple.

The part of the law that talks about financial abuse says:

"Financial abuse" of an elder or dependent adult occurs when a person or entity does any of the following:

1. Takes, secretes, appropriates, or retains real or personal property of an elder or dependent adult to a wrongful use or with intent to defraud, or both.

2. Assists in taking, secreting, appropriating, or retaining real or personal property of an elder or dependent adult to a wrongful use or with intent to defraud, or both.

"A person or entity shall be deemed to have taken, secreted, appropriated, or retained property for a wrongful use if, among other things, the person or entity takes, secretes, appropriates, or retains possession of property in bad faith."[1]

To put this in lay-person terms, abuse means hurting, neglecting, or doing harm to an elder. When it comes to finances, it includes what we might think of as ripping off an elder, stealing their property or money, committing fraud to get their money or property, or influencing them in a way that takes unfair advantage and harms them.

Donald and His Caregiver

Donald was an eighty-year-old widowed man with early dementia. He had been a CEO of a large and successful company. He was a tall, bossy, and imposing man in a younger day, and his family was intimidated by him. As he began to lose his independence, his family moved him to a high-end, elegant assisted living facility.

Donald was a wealthy man, as was everyone in the facility. One of the caregivers "befriended" Donald, establishing a close relationship with him. She was very affectionate with Donald, to the point that she should have been questioned by her employer.

She eventually persuaded Donald to wire $10,000 to her boyfriend in a foreign country, and, on an outing with her, he did so.

Donald's family was furious. He saw nothing wrong with what had happened. He said he loved the caregiver and wanted to help her. The family expressed their outrage over the incident to the assisted living facility, but did not report the caregiver or the facility to the state to prosecute the crime.

UNDUE INFLUENCE

Donald's case is a good example of the issue of *undue influence*. That means using one's position of trust to manipulate another for the manipulator's good and not for the benefit of the elder. The caregiver was in a position of trust. Donald had been lonely since his wife died, and the caregiver knew it and took advantage of her position. She intentionally got close and spent a lot of time with him. She took him on outings, and they had fun. The entire time her purpose was to get at his money.

Many states have a clear definition of undue influence as a part of elder abuse, but some do not. The problem with not having a clear legal definition of this kind of manipulation is that it becomes harder to prosecute. In Donald's case, as in many cases, legal authorities were never involved.

Donald liked the facility, and this was a factor in the family's choice not to report the caregiver to the police. Had the family pressed charges, and if the local District Attorney had sufficient evidence, the caregiver, the caregiver's employer, the home's administration, and facility's owners could have been prosecuted. It is clearly a crime under the law to manipulate a man with dementia into giving money to a stranger in another country. However, the caregiver actually got away with it, in this case.

The National Center on Elder Abuse has extensive data and research studies on how prevalent abuse is and how often it is reported. Their site tells us of studies showing major financial exploitation in 41 out of 1,000 elders. Most abusers are family members. Most cases of abuse are unreported.

Although abuse can occur in many forms, when we look at financial abuse, we may have more clear ways to prevent it—in my opinion—than some other forms of elder abuse. Money leaves a trail—it can be tracked. Dates of transactions can be obtained from banks and other financial custodians. We can measure assets, gains, and losses in a much more tangible way than we can measure emotional damage to an elder.

WHAT MAKES OUR AGING PARENTS VULNERABLE TO ABUSE?

One of the most common reasons why our loved ones are abused and sometimes wiped out financially is because of isolation and loneliness.

As they age, physical problems can reduce the opportunity to socialize. Many elders lose the ability to drive, which may happen gradually. As an example, my mother-in-law, Alice, is ninety-two and still drives, but not at night. She voluntarily gave up night driving because it was hard for her to see the road at night. This has definitely limited what she can do in the evenings. If she wants to go out to dinner, she is dependent on friends to take her. So far, she has managed, but if the friend who does the driving also loses the ability to drive at night, she will be even more isolated. She will have to find another way to get around. With age, finding new friends can also become increasingly difficult.

Mobility may be reduced as an elder ages. Hearing is more likely to be impaired. Friends become ill and die, and the social circle narrows. This kind of isolation makes the elder a perfect target for a scammer, con artist, or any thief who has intentionally developed the skill of preying on the vulnerable. They are very successful as thieves because most financial abuse cases are not reported.

Death of a Spouse

When you lose a parent, you may be deeply affected by your own grief, and you may not realize that your other parent (or step-parent or grandparent) is automatically a target for scammers and thieves. Remember that birth and death records are public. The county where your loved one resides publishes these statistics daily. Anyone can search for deaths, find out who the survivors are from the obituary, and target the widow or widower as prospective prey. This may happen soon after the passing of the other spouse, while the elder is most shaky and least able to see a predator coming.

This is especially true if your loved one moves to a new place, has to adjust to new people and surroundings, or is otherwise lonely. The risk can increase further because of the need for a friend. Scammers know this well and fish for victims all over this country every day. They work their way into a person's life, and the elder looks forward to the contact and feels cared about, even to the point of an addiction. These thieves want to create dependency on the part of the elder. Once established, this kind of addiction tends to not be amenable to reason or persuasion by concerned family. Newly "befriended" elders crave the contact and do not want to cut it off.

Remember that death of a spouse is a signal event. Not only does it radically change your loved one's life, but it also makes your loved one a sitting duck if no one is paying attention.

Roy's Story

Roy's wife had cancer for three years, and he spent a lot of time caring for her. When she died, he was eighty-three years old. He already had some signs of early dementia—including memory loss—but he was still competent in many areas to make decisions.

He was estranged from his two adult children who had numerous difficult disagreements with him in prior years. After their mother died, they more or less ignored Roy. He felt a pervasive sadness and felt lost. However, a woman he knew at his local grocery store, Betty, who waited on him frequently, didn't ignore him. She started coming by to see him and "console" him within a week of his wife's death.

One month after his wife died, Betty moved into Roy's house. She showered him with affection and cooked for him. Before long, she told him how her credit card debt of $300,000 was crushing her, and she wondered if he might give her a loan. She told him she could pay it back with an inheritance she was about to receive, so he wrote her a check.

She disappeared.

The police were called, and a case was opened, but there was no chance that Roy was going to get his money back. It had been spent. Clearly, the situation was a combination of factors, starting with the estranged relationship between Roy and his children. Their avoidance made Roy's loneliness worse after his wife passed. Betty was an opportunist who knew exactly what to do to get Roy's money, and she succeeded.

One thing we can learn from this story is that the death of a spouse puts an elder in a vulnerable position. If family avoids the elder for any reason, the problem is worse. There are countless dysfunctional families whose members do not get along. However, unless you are so cold as to be okay with the vulnerable elder possibly being left destitute and homeless, please pay attention to this situation when it happens in your family. The right thing to do is to check in and watch out for a sudden showing of inordinate interest by a supposed new friend or an old acquaintance of your aging loved one. If you think there is an ulterior motive, there just might be.

Isolation and the Internet

Because of the decreasing opportunities for social life, loss of spouses and friends, and the scattering of families all over, the problems of isolation increase. Lonely people are at risk for a lot of problems, and financial abuse is certainly among them.

When an elder's main activity is watching TV and he does not get out much, he becomes a convenient and easy target for telephone scammers. If he is on the Internet, it is likewise true that he is a target and could fall victim readily. Elders want and need contact. Trained, clever thieves know just how to provide it.

Scammers may call after the death of a spouse or as a result of buying a list of names from a magazine publisher or sweepstakes company. If one got a list of every subscriber to the Reader's Digest, for example, there are sure to be plenty of elders on it. Some sweepstakes companies collect names and ages of ticket buyers, as well as addresses. If the thieves keep dialing those phone numbers, they are sure to find prey before long. There is no law against selling the names and contact information collected by magazine sales or sweepstakes entrants to the highest bidder.

The scammers are invariably friendly and patient. They offer to listen, ask pleasant questions, and make up identities that sound plausible. A lonely widow might need someone to talk to. She may enjoy the seeming kindness of the salesman. Gradually, they build a relationship and stay in frequent contact. The request for money comes at a carefully strategized time when the victim is deemed *ready*.

Victims do not see how their own isolation is setting them up for these schemes—they comply. The requests get more aggressive and are sometimes accompanied by threats—it works. It may not stop until someone, such as a concerned family member, can persuade the elder to stop the contact or when bank accounts are drained.

With the Internet, it can be even worse. Thieves can make up identities, even if they barely speak English. They can easily lie and readily escape detection. There is no caller

ID, and their Internet addresses can be disguised to look real or official, or even appear to be from the government.

The Warren Family

Natalie called my office in great distress. She lived at a distance from her father, age ninety. For years, he had lived on a large ranch in his country home, rather far from anyone. After his wife passed away, his adult children encouraged him to learn to use a computer. He did learn and discovered a world on the Internet.

Natalie told me that her father had been giving money to someone posing as a representative from an African refugee organization alleging to be rescuing desperate people from gangs. She had discovered—to her dismay and horror—that he had given over $100,000 to these impostors over a period of at least a year.

She and her siblings had confronted their father, saying that he was being defrauded. He just told them, "You don't understand." He believed that he would be recognized as a hero and would get a large reward for his good deeds.

The Internet thieves were people with whom he had a relationship, which he thought was a friendship. They emailed him multiple times a day. When they asked for money, he had it sent from his bank. He was essentially addicted to the contact.

I urged Natalie to report the financial abuse to authorities, but she and her siblings did not want to embarrass their father. After all, he was a wealthy ranch owner and had a reputation. When I asked them why they did not take more assertive steps to protect their father, since they had the legal means to do, Natalie said that she and her sisters "didn't want to upset him."

I never heard a worse excuse for allowing financial abuse to go on unchecked. Fortunately, with some urging on my part, the family stepped up its efforts to get their father to give up his position of control over most of his assets by stepping down as trustee of two trusts. It took two months to get this done, and the Internet thieves continued to get Natalie's father to give them money during the protracted negotiations. Taking a more assertive stance with her father when she first noticed the harm could have stopped the con artists much sooner.

Cognitive Impairment

According to The National Center on Elder Abuse, 2.9 billion dollars a year is stolen from elders, and those with dementia are at high risk. A recent non-government study puts the annual figure for the same demographic much higher: 36.5 billion dollars.

The idea of cognitive impairment or mental decline is a difficult one for most of us to accept. One of its most difficult aspects is that it comes on slowly, insidiously, and more or less sneaks up on the person affected.

Normal aging does not include mental decline. Though many or most of us take a little longer to process complex information as we age, if we do not have brain disease, we are still as intellectually capable as we were when we were younger. Those elders whose brains remain healthy throughout life do not automatically have cognitive impairment just because they are older.

On the other hand, brain disease in the form of Alzheimer's disease (often referred to as dementia), affects about one in three people over age eighty-five. It has many warning signs, which include memory loss, changes in judgment, and difficulty with words and familiar tasks.

Cognitive impairment makes a person vulnerable to abuse because financial judgment may be one of the very first areas of function to be affected. The person with early cognitive impairment may seem fine on the outside. She may be able to carry on a normal conversation. She may be able to pay bills on time or to discuss politics. The subtle damage does not show at first.

When the early warning signs do emerge, the family may dismiss them, thinking he's just getting old or everyone forgets sometimes. Be warned: If you think you are seeing red flag warnings that something is wrong with your loved one, there probably is something wrong. For example, it is not normal for a man who has been living in the same house for fifty years to get lost going home by what should be a familiar route. It is not part of "just getting old;" it is not a regular part of aging; it doesn't happen to everyone; and it may well be a sign that there is a problem.

Getting lost in familiar places is an ominous sign of brain changes that can mean your loved one is at great risk for financial abuse. However, there can be other reasons for these behavioral changes. New medications, combinations of medications, medical conditions, or events such as stroke can all affect behavior. If you see warning signs and you are in a position to request it, you can ask your loved one to see a doctor to find out the causes. An examination can help give everyone the information you need to take protective action or not.

Telephone and Internet scammers are raking in the spoils of their fraud and lies in increasing numbers because there are more elders now than ever and it is a crime of opportunity. A cognitively impaired person can't see a scam coming. What might be obviously phony to you or to me might sound very good to an impaired person. But one need not be impaired to be gullible. Other motives can also influence elders to become victims.

Fear of Running out of Money

The oldest members of our population have lived through the Great Depression and have also seen a major downturn in the recent Great Recession. As this is written, we have not fully recovered from the effects of the recession. It has affected many elders who depend on interest on their investments to make ends meet. They fear running out of money and may be surprised by their living so long.

They probably didn't calculate having to make retirement savings last into their nineties and beyond.

When a clever and skilled con artist finds any elder who is afraid of running out of cash to live on, he gets to the elder by pointing out how low the returns are in banks, CDs, and other low-interest paying investments. He offers a "great deal," sometimes guaranteeing the elder a high return. He uses a trusting relationship or a friendly manner to draw in the elder.

Nigel's Story

Nigel was an accomplished professional who had retired from a successful career with a good-sized nest egg. He and his wife traveled and enjoyed leisure pursuits. When he turned eighty-eight, he began to do some calculations. His wife was having some health problems, and they were going to have to hire help for her. This is not covered by Medicare. He grew concerned about the high cost of care.

His financial advisor had been in his life for only a few years, and Nigel believed in him. In good times, his advice to Nigel had paid off well. Now, with the recession concerning Nigel, the advisor asked Nigel to invest in a real estate project, promising huge returns. The advisor was putting his own money in as well, he told Nigel. Nigel gave him $300,000 to invest. Interest payments came in for about four months.

Then they stopped.

Suddenly, Nigel could not reach the advisor. The

recording on the office phone said he had moved, but gave no new address.

I met Nigel at a Legal Aid clinic where I was volunteering to give free legal advice to the community. I gave Nigel some advice and referred him to a specialist attorney who could follow up after the clinic. The sad outcome was that Nigel was probably not going to ever see his $300,000 again.

Nigel was not a person with poor judgment, but his fear of running out of money caused him to do something foolish. There was poor documentation for the investment in the real estate project. It was very high risk and not suitable for a person of Nigel's age or position. It was an inappropriate gamble for Nigel. His choice was driven by fear.

There Is No Law Against Stupid Decisions

We are not talking about dementia, nor recent loss of a spouse. We are not seeing cognitive impairment in this next story. People sometimes make foolish, irrational choices based on emotion.

Petra's Story

In this story, we see a path to abuse that a family member managed to stop in its tracks. It is hard to explain how it came to be.

Petra's mother, Katia, and she were very close. Petra was her mother's agent on the Durable Power of Attorney, and she stayed in close touch with Katia, age ninety. Katia was a retired accountant, always good with figures and bookkeeping. Petra worked part time as a counselor and did not make very much money. Petra's husband was disabled, and Petra's mother generously gave them a cash gift each year to help out.

Katia developed some mobility problems, but she wanted to take yoga. Petra found a yoga teacher for her, one who would come to Katia's home.

The yoga teacher, Luis, a South American, was charming and attentive. Katia loved it and got very accustomed to doing yoga at home twice a week. Things seemed fine for several months until Petra learned that Katia was planning to take a cruise ship to South America—where she had never had any desire to go before—and was going to take Luis with her. She had already paid her deposit.

Petra was very hesitant to suggest to her mother that something wasn't right with her relationship with Luis. After all, Petra depended on her mom for some of her financial support. Her mother did not see how easy it would be for Luis to simply use Katia for a free ride in luxury to his home country, where he would likely just get off the ship at the first port and leave Katia stunned at his disappearance. It looked and felt like a setup.

When I consulted with Petra, I urged her to point out to her mother how a cruise ship was not at all like what

Katia had ever wanted to do and that there were signs that Luis was pushing her. I suggested that Petra warn her mother that nothing would prevent Luis from abandoning her once in his home territory. I also advised her to speak directly to Luis and warn him that she was watching his every move. Petra did and Luis, fortunately, backed off the plan. They were lucky. It could have turned out very differently.

Eventually, Luis quit the job, and Petra found Katia another, local, yoga teacher. It was a close call. Luis seemed to have designs on one thing: A free ride back home, but he well could have been after much more of Katia's assets. Katia's apparently dumb decision to go along with the cruise ship idea was out of character for her. Her close, trusting relationship with Petra was key to stopping what looked like elder abuse in the making. Fortunately, she was willing to listen to her daughter.

No matter how intelligent, accomplished, or powerful your aging parent was, things can change. Intelligence is not a guaranteed protection against elder abuse. Some very bright people get taken by scams every day. They may be emotionally vulnerable at the time it happens. They may have grown more isolated when you weren't paying attention. They may be at risk for things you never imagined.

Your appropriate and well-meaning efforts to help them find social connections can backfire and set them up for danger.

Can we stop the scams and con artists? We can't control risky situations, but we can raise our own awareness and pay closer attention to our aging loved ones. If we maintain frequent contact, we at least have a better chance of warding off abuse before it is too late to stop it.

WHAT CAN A RESPONSIBLE FAMILY DO TO PREVENT FINANCIAL ABUSE?

As you can see from these true stories of what happened to these families, one protection is to stay in close contact with your elder. This is a personal decision. It is made all the more difficult if you have a strained relationship with your elder.

Some families have a parent who was not a good parent, or who was outright abusive or bullying when their children were growing up. Some families report that verbally abusive parents continue to be verbally abusive, even as they are growing very old and frail. It's a personality trait that doesn't go away for these elders.

Unpleasant people are the ones everyone wants to stay away from, yet, as they become vulnerable for a number of reasons, they need more supervision rather than less. Are there ways to manage this? I think so.

Have the Necessary Conversations

One of the first steps in dealing with an unpleasant older person in your life who may need help is to initiate the necessary conversation. The *what ifs* have to be talked about to explore what the elder wants and what you can tolerate. For example, you would need to ask, "What if you had a stroke and couldn't talk? What would you want to do? Who would you want to take care of you?"

Most people don't care to talk about becoming infirm and needing help, because it is too hard to imagine being dependent on others and losing control—they avoid it. But if you know you can't stand being around an elder and you don't want to be the one to do any caregiving, you will need to bring up the question and, if care is needed, determine how the elder would pay for it.

When there are enough funds on hand to hire the necessary help, manage money, pay bills, and balance the checkbook, you can work on an agreement about that. If there are not enough funds to pay for help, you and your elder need to explore the possibility of public benefits, government funded programs, low-cost senior services in the area, and volunteer groups.

In one community that I checked into recently for a sixty-five-year-old, low-income stroke victim, I found a free *Friendly Visitors* program where vetted volunteers will visit the elder for at least an hour every week to keep an eye on things. They can report to family so that the family is informed without being directly involved in finding out how the elder is doing.

Get Your Paperwork in Order

Another step for every family, whether you get along with your elder or not, is to request that the elder see an estate planning attorney and get the basic legal documents done. There is often resistance because seeing a lawyer costs money. If your elder has low income, free or low-cost legal services may be available. In my own community, any person age sixty-five or older can use free Legal Aid, regardless of income level. Volunteer attorneys do basic work such as creating wills and simple trusts, preparing a durable power of attorney, and outlining an advance healthcare directive.

Why are these documents important to prevent elder abuse? Every competently drawn up trust has a provision in it that tells the elder what will happen if she becomes incapacitated for making financial decisions. It will name someone the elder has chosen to take over when the time comes. That gives a person, under the specific circumstances that are spelled out in the trust, the right to take over financial management of the trust money or property. Getting this successor in place can stop others from ripping off an elder who has dementia or is otherwise lacking in sound judgment about finances.

It is not a perfect solution, but getting essential legal

documents signed is better than no solution and no planning, which is how most people find themselves when abuse happens.

A Durable Power of Attorney, as mentioned in the first chapter, is a way to stop elder abuse. If your elder trusts you and is willing to admit to the need for help, this document will permit someone else, usually a relative, to protect the elder from abuse by controlling the checking account and other assets. With proper use of a DPOA, you can literally take the funds away from an elder who is at risk for abuse and keep them where neither she nor the abuser can get them.

Again, this is far from perfect. Just as a DPOA can protect an elder, it can also be revoked at the urging and undue influence of an abuser. The abuser can get control over funds with misuse of the document by getting the elder to sign a new one.

There are alternatives to using family as the agent on a DPOA or on a trust. Some elders simply don't trust their relatives. The agent on a DPOA, or even on a trust, is usually a family member, but it doesn't have to be. It can be a trusted friend or a licensed professional, called a fiduciary. It is important to make the effort to get your loved ones to sign a DPOA in case you need it. They do help in many cases. They save families from having to go to court for a guardianship. The benefits outweigh the risks by far.

Stay in Contact, Either in Person or Through Others

Make personal visits. What you think is going on in a phone call may be very different from what you see face-to-face. If you get along with your loved one, make scheduled personal visits as often as you can manage it. If you have trouble with this, perhaps another relative could fill in for you, or a volunteer could be arranged to report to you on a weekly basis. If you have willing siblings, you may be able to rotate and share the load.

If you notice from all of the stories in this chapter, the worst situations occurred when the elder was isolated from family for long periods of time. In the one example where the aging mother, Katia, was saved from what looked like brewing abuse, it was her trusting relationship with her daughter that saved her and probably prevented a much worse situation.

Introduce Technology and Online Banking

Although the majority of seniors are not using the Internet, it is possible for an elder to learn to use it. When this happens, it can do a great deal to reduce isolation and allow frequent contact with an elderly family member. It may take a lot of encouragement on your part as an adult child. Grandchildren can also be a great help. Use of the Internet by an elder has risks—as Internet fraud is rampant—but you can teach your loved one to be aware of fraud, use Internet safety, and never give out personal information to anyone who solicits it.

Even if your loved one does not want to do online banking, you can still get his permission to access the account online. This can be done with his written permission in a limited power of attorney for banks and financial institutions, stock brokerages, etc. That is a protection that will allow you to see suspicious activity as soon as it happens. My husband looks at his mom's account every month and gets paper statements from the financial manager as well.

The bank or institution provides the document they use to share signing power. This document must be notarized, which they also do at the institution. An outside DPOA is supposed to allow you to access information from a loved one's account if you are named as the agent on the DPOA, but many banks refuse to recognize what your state otherwise lets you do, and they may force you to get the bank's power of attorney signed for them separately. If you want to monitor or access your aging parent's bank accounts, be aware of this, and get it done at the time any other documents, such as a DPOA, are being signed. Otherwise, you may think you've done everything right, only to find out that the bank is resisting your efforts to watch over an aging parent.

Alice at Eighty-Six

My mother-in-law, Alice, refused to touch a computer while her husband was alive. After she was widowed, she realized that she couldn't pay her own bills without the help of her adult children—that was not okay. She's very independent, so my husband was able to persuade her to learn how to do online banking.

The added benefit is that my husband shares the signing power on her accounts, since he is the agent she appointed on her DPOA. He also has access to her accounts and can monitor everything she does. If he has a question about spending, he asks her. My husband uses remote access software to be able to log into her computer from a distance, and he can even check her banking activity from his smart phone. She is well protected against any potential Internet or other con artists.

PROTECTIVE MEASURES

The protective measures I suggest here apply to parents whose company you may enjoy as well as those whom you avoid. If you have a problem closely watching over an aging relative with whom you do not get along, you will certainly need someone else to help you. A neighbor whom you trust, a clergy person, or trusted financial advisor can all be part of the solution to protecting a vulnerable aging person with whom your own communications are less than ideal. Above all, you do not want to ignore an aging parent's vulnerability because you do not get along well. If he gets abused financially, he could be left with no money at all, as sometimes does happen. That is a worse problem than finding a way to monitor a difficult parent.

I recommend the following steps for all our aging family members.

Talk with Your Aging Parent About Financial Abuse

Your parents need to be made aware of how to protect themselves as much as possible. Simply making them aware is not enough, but it is a start.

There are many resources available to help you educate them about scams. One good place for information is the previously mentioned National Center on Elder Abuse. Local senior centers also sponsor live programs specifically directed to elders on scams and how to thwart them. Local county and state governments have taken up the cause of working harder to stop elder abuse. Watch for programs offered in your loved one's community. The federal government has recently put more funding into education about elder abuse in an effort to help both professionals, such as lawyers, and the general public become more aware.

A helpful resource in the federal government is the Consumer Financial Protection Bureau. They put excellent information together in a consumer-oriented, download-able booklet titled, "Managing Someone Else's Money." This booklet is designed for those who are agents under a Durable Power of Attorney, though it can be useful for anyone. It describes what you can and can't do if you are responsible for handling finances for anyone else and pro-vides a good list of common scams. We recommend it as a high quality source of information about elder financial abuse prevention. It is also useful in that it describes what to do if an elder has been financially abused, where to go for help, and how to report abuse.

At my website, AgingParents.com, we discuss five of the common scams discussed in the booklet. We have created short animated films anyone can use to learn about these five scams.

Educate Yourself

You can't be vigilant about your aging loved one and try to protect them from scams if you don't know the scammers' moves yourself. There are classics that have been around for a long time, such as sweepstakes scams, and there are new Internet thieves constantly trolling for victims. Work at staying abreast of the latest scams affecting elders.

Start Early with More Frequent Contact

If your parent is past his seventieth birthday and seems to be perfectly okay, it does not mean that he will always be capable of protecting against elder abuse. The professional crooks who prey on elders know more tricks and schemes to draw in their victims than we can even imagine. Even if you have not been in the habit of calling your aging relative every week, it is a good idea to start this habit now. Visiting with the intention of checking on their finances is also a good protective move. They may resist this idea, but it is important to stay involved if you are allowed to do so by the elders in your family. Keep trying, and keep asking tactful questions. Tell them about schemes against elders that make the news. You can be sure that if you have none to talk about offhand, that a brief bit of Internet research on the subject of victims of elder abuse will lead to many stories from across the country. One will never run out of anecdotes, and talking about them is a good way to tactfully educate an elder.

Snoop a Bit

This may sound like an intrusion. This may not sit well with everyone. This may offend your aging loved one if they know about your actions, but I advocate for doing it anyway. There is too much at stake to avoid being informed as to what your aging loved ones are doing with their finances. If we did not have a widespread problem with elder abuse, no one would have to monitor it. But we do have a problem, and there is no way to learn about what is going on with an aging parent unless you or someone you can count on is closely watching over them. This might mean checking their email from time to time if you can.

We discussed a family whose father, living alone in the country, was being scammed through emails. He received dozens of them a day, asking him to give money to a fake cause, which had stolen thousands of dollars from him by the time the family found out about it. If family members had not looked at his email (in this case, with his permission), they never would have known what was going on. Even if they had checked his email without his permission, they at least had a starting place to begin all efforts to take protective action from that point on. Ultimately, they took major steps to take control over most of his money.

Check the Mail from Time to Time As Well

If charitable appeals are frequent and your aging parent is giving money to all of them, they will have him on every list in existence and will repeatedly ask for more money. Be suspicious if you see dozens of charity appeal letters in your loved one's mail. Older people who do not use the

Internet are often victimized by mail. Some of the charities are legitimate and some are not. But a person with
memory loss may not recall how many checks she has
written to any given charity, and it is important to keep
watch over the giving. Charities can also scam and take
advantage of elders; I have witnessed this more than once
with my own clients.

A FINAL WORD OF CAUTION

Most financial abuse occurs at the hands of family members. If you are a witness to this, you will need to find the
courage to report it in an effort to end the abuse. Many
people, including the elders themselves, are very reluctant
to report abuse by a family member. If you see suspicious
signs and have some evidence of abuse to report, the place
to start is with Adult Protective Services (APS) in the
county where the abuse is believed to have occurred.

Reporting elder abuse commits you to providing whatever information you can to APS. You do need to name
names, give examples of what you believe happened,
explain why you think it happened and provide dates, or
give approximate periods during which suspicious activity occurred. Because this is such an emotionally charged
issue and elders may not want to cooperate, it can make
things difficult for law enforcement. I encourage you to

at least take the step of reporting abuse if you believe it is going on. Adult Protective Services may or may not proceed with a case after the activity is reported, but at least you can say that you have done your part.

SUMMARY

Elder abuse in the United States is a growing 36.5-billion-dollars-a-year problem. Elders may be vulnerable due to many factors, of which cognitive impairment is the most pressing issue. It alters a person's judgment to the point that she cannot see a scam coming and may be completely unable to recognize the risk of being abused financially.

Emotional factors are also a part of the picture of risk. These include loneliness—particularly after the loss of a spouse—physical isolation due to impaired mobility, loss of one's accustomed social circle, as well as depression and grief. Clever thieves seize the opportunity to exploit elders who are vulnerable and to take every advantage of them.

Intelligence is no protection against financial abuse. Educated and accomplished older people can fall victim. The critical steps for you to take include educating your loved one, educating yourself, monitoring your aging parents as much as possible, and simply paying attention to what is going on with their financial lives.

Educating our loved ones and ourselves is essential to stopping abuse.

Elder abuse is a crime of opportunity. Watching over our aging parents and keeping in mind the risks can do much to keep them financially safe.

Recommended Resources

- "Managing Someone Else's Money." http://files. ConsumerFinance.gov/f/201310_cfpb_lay_fiduciary_ guides_guardians.pdf. Consumer Financial Protection Bureau. Accessed November 15, 2014.

- "5 Financial scams that target your aging loved ones." *Youtube* video. http://Youtu.be/LQlCe-W6rbk. Accessed January 9, 2015.

ENDNOTES

*CHAPTER 1: What You Need to Know About
Finances and Aging Loved Ones*

1. Daniel Marson, "Impact of Dementia on Capacity
   to Manage Finances and Prevention of Financial
   Exploitation" (presentation, University of Iowa, Iowa
   City, IA, March 1, 2012).

*CHAPTER 2: The Path to Peace in Family
Arguments About Aging Parents*

1. Steven R. Marsh, "The Truths Behind Mediation," Last
   modified in 2000, adrr.com/adr3/other.htm, (last
   accessed 10/31/14), Mediate Resolution Services,
   accessed October 31, 2014. www.Mediate.com.

CHAPTER 3: Aging Parents and Giving Up Driving

1. Robert J. Derocher, "Licensing Older Drivers: Renewed
   Calls for In-Person Testing," *Experience, Senior
   Lawyers Division American Bar Association* 18, no. 2
   (Winter 2008): 13–16.

CHAPTER 5: Will You Need to Help Your Aging Parents Financially?

1. "The Market for Long-Term Care Insurance," www. NBER.org/bah/winter05/w10989.html, National Bureau of Economic Research, accessed November 12, 2014.
2. "2013 Alzheimer's Disease Facts and Figures," www.ALZ.org/downloads/facts_figures_2013.pdf, Alzheimer's Association, accessed 11/13/14.

CHAPTER 6: Taking Your Aging Parent into Your Home

1. "Family and Medical Leave Act," www.dol.gov/dol/ topic/benefits-leave/fmla.htm, US Department of Labor.

CHAPTER 10: Protecting Our Aging Loved Ones from Abuse

1. California Welfare and Institutions Code, Sec. § 15657.6 et seq.

APPENDIX A

Texas Aging Network: Senior Driving Assessment Checklist

If you are concerned about an older driver's safety on the road, the best way to evaluate his or her driving ability is to ride along with them. Use the checklist below to record your observations after (not during) your ride. If you can, ask several people to take rides at different times of the day.

☐ Ran a red light

☐ Ignored or misinterpreted traffic lights, stop signs, or yield signs

☐ Did not appear to notice other vehicles, pedestrians, bicycles, or road hazards

☐ Had a near miss

☐ Had difficulty physically while driving (did not look over shoulder or to the rear when appropriate, or had trouble turning the wheel)

☐ Did not look or yield when pulling out of parking space or driveway

☐ Crossed into other lanes when driving straight

☐ Drove too close to the car ahead

☐ Did not stay in lane when turning

☐ Drove aggressively

☐ Drove too slowly

☐ Stopped inappropriately

☐ Did not signal correctly

☐ Did not anticipate potential danger or changing traffic conditions (slowing down when brake lights appeared ahead)

☐ Ran over a curb

☐ Asked passengers whether the road was clear

☐ Became frustrated or irritated

☐ Appeared confused or frightened

☐ Parked inappropriately

If you checked any of the six items in the "Gray Zone," your older driver should be prevented from driving, at least temporarily, while you further investigate.

Next Steps in Assessing Driving Ability and Safety

First, have your older driver's vision and hearing tested. Schedule a complete physical examination where the doctor will pay particular attention to physical reflexes and any medications that might be contributing to confusion or drowsiness.

If you are certain that your driver is a danger behind the wheel and should not be driving, as a last resort, you can make a report to your parents' state Department of Motor Vehicles. The report is in the form of a *Request for Reexamination,* which can result in the Department asking the driver to come in and go through the written and behind-the-wheel tests.

Additional Resources for Elders and Driving

American Automobile Association (AAA)

AAA.exchange.com

AAA Roadwise Review: A Tool to Help Seniors Drive Safely Longer: SeniorDriving. AAA.com/evaluate-your-driving-ability/ interactive-driving-evaluation

A computer-based screening tool allows seniors to measure the eight functional abilities shown to be the strongest predictors of crash risk among older drivers. They can use this at home.

AAA.com

Enter your ZIP code to be redirected to the AAA club in your area. Look for a Mature Operator Driving Refresher course. This could help your client extend driving longer than he might without the course.

AAA Foundation for Traffic Safety: AAAfoundation.org

Quizzes, tips, and information for older drivers, including a searchable database of local transportation options. This may be a critical part of the discussion about how to get around after giving up the keys.

American Association of Motor Vehicle Administrators (AAMVA)

AAMVA.org

State-by-state contacts for information on driver's licensing, reporting unsafe drivers, and services for seniors.

American Association of Retired Persons (AARP)

AARP.org/home-garden/transportation/driver_safety

This Driver Safety refresher course is a new version of what used to be the "55-Alive" driver refresher course. Locate a nearby course at the link above.

American Medical Association (AMA)

AMA-ASSN.org/ama/pub/physi-cian-resources/public-health/promot-ing-healthy-lifestyles/geriatric-health.page

Access several resources, including the Physician's Guide to Assessing and Counseling Older Drivers, developed by the American Medical Association in cooperation with the National Highway Traffic Safety Administration.

American Occupational Therapy Association (AOTA)

AOTA.org/olderdriver

Find an occupational therapist who is a driver rehabilitation specialist. They do driving evaluations to find out if a person is competent to drive or if they can be rehabilitated to become a safer driver.

National Association of Area Agencies on Aging (n4a)

n4a.org

This is a federally funded general resource for senior services, including transportation services.

APPENDIX B

Interview Questions to Use When Considering a Home Care Agency

In preparing this section, I interviewed several home care provider agencies. I have also worked with their owners on various community education projects. This list of questions is a compilation of materials offered from owners as well as my own additions to the material.

1. How long has your agency been in business? Can you tell me about the backgrounds of the owners and directors? (Many new agencies are springing up because of the vastly growing elderly population. Some are opened by people who have absolutely no experience or credentials to work with this population. Longevity in the business often signals a good reputation.)

2. What organizations in the community do you work with (i.e., hospitals, Alzheimer's Association, Hospice, etc.)? Do you have references in these organizations? Are there other references that you can give for your agency?

3. How do you find your caregivers? What kind of experience do you require of your staff? Do you train your workers? What kind of certifications do your staff members hold?

4. Can you tell me about the screening process you use in hiring your workers? Do you conduct background checks? What kind of check do you do? Do you have them go through an orientation process? Do you have ongoing training for your staff?

5. Are the workers in your agency employees or independent contractors? (Employees cost more but are supervised—I recommend going with an agency that classifies their workers as such.)

6. Are taxes, insurances, and workers' compensation handled by your agency? Do you pay the caregiver, or is that our responsibility?

7. Will someone come out to do an initial assessment? Is there a charge for that service?

8. Tell me how the scheduling works; are there any time minimums? Do we have to commit to a certain amount of service?

9. What if something comes up and we need to cancel; how flexible is your cancellation policy?

10. Can we expect the same caregiver each time?

11. What is your agency's course of action if our care-giver is sick or unable to work for some reason?

12. Is it possible to reach an agency representative after business hours or on the weekends?

13. What if we have a last minute need; can you help us?

14. What is your agency's course of action if the care-giver is not working out?

15. How do you manage your staff once you assign them?

16. Do you offer care management? Is there a charge for those services?

17. Please tell me about insurances that your agency carries. Are your employees insured and bonded?

18. Can the staff drive my elder to run errands? Do they drive in their own cars, or can they drive my parent's vehicle? How does insurance factor in?

19. What can I expect the caregiver to do? What can't they do?

20. What can I expect from your agency in terms of communication?

21. Does your staff keep written care logs? How often are those reviewed? Will I be able to see and review them? Are they online? Are they on the cloud?

22. How often will an agency representative visit my mom or dad to check on things?

23. My mom has long-term care insurance; do you work with these policies? How much assistance will you provide in filing her claim and assuring that all the paperwork is taken care of? Will you directly bill insurance companies?

24. Do your workers handle money for my loved one? Do they take care of shopping? How do you ensure that they are handling money in a safe way?

APPENDIX C

Ten Things to Look for When Checking Out a Nursing Home

If you can, always check out any skilled nursing facility (rehabilitation center or nursing home) in person before sending a loved one there. Safety is the greatest concern. Here is my checklist of things to notice and ask about:

1. Go there unannounced. You can ask for a tour when you get there. Not telling them in advance gives you a chance to see how things are on a typical day.

2. Note whether there is someone at the front desk. Security is important. If no one is in attendance, it's not a good sign. If they want you to sign in, that's helpful.

3. What is your first impression? Does it look, feel, or smell bad? Or does it seem like a decent and friendly atmosphere?

4. Are there a lot of residents lined up along the walls in wheelchairs, doing nothing?

5. Do you see any staff around you? Understaffing is an ongoing problem in nursing homes. You can ask

about how many aides work there during the day-time and how many residents each one takes care of.

6. If you walk the corridors, look into a room and see if there are water pitchers nearby the beds. Dehydration is a serious problem in nursing homes, and the residents should have ready access to drinking water or other beverages.

7. If you are taken on a tour, ask how long the director has been there. Ask how long the social worker has been there. High staff turnover is a problem and can lead to breakdown in consistent care of the residents.

8. Ask to see the entire facility, including the recreation room, dining room, and any other common areas for residents.

9. Ask about activity programs. Some homes have recreational and exercise therapists who help keep residents engaged. Entertainment is offered from time to time at the best homes with singing and other musical performances. If they have none, it is not a good sign.

10. Ask about what therapy is offered, how often it is available, and how many therapists are on staff. This includes physical, occupational, and speech therapy. Some facilities also offer recreational therapy,, which may include art and music as well as exercise therapy.

ABOUT THE AUTHOR

CAROLYN ROSENBLATT is a Baby Boomer author with an aging parent. She grew up in a large family in suburban Los Angeles, California. She spent ten years nursing, working primarily with elders and their families. While practicing nursing, she worked her way through law school.

Carolyn's law career spanned twenty-seven years, with twenty-five years in her own practice. She then started AgingParents.com in 2006 with her husband, psychologist Dr. Mikol Davis, with the aim to be a resource for those who have aging loved ones. Carolyn and Mikol work together every day, consulting with adult children who have aging parents or mediating their disputes. You can get help for your aging parent problems, or request speaking engagements at AgingParents.com, 930 Irwin St., Suite 215, San Rafael, CA 94901, (866) 962-4464, or via email at clrosenblatt@gmail.com or drmikol@agingparents.com. Carolyn lives with her husband in San Rafael, California. They have two wonderful, grown children.

ABOUT FAMILIUS

Welcome to a place where mothers are celebrated, not compared. Where heart is at the center of our families, and family at the center of our homes. Where boo boos are still kissed, cake beaters are still licked, and mistakes are still okay. Welcome to a place where books—and family—are beautiful. Familius: a book publisher dedicated to helping families be happy.

Visit Our Website: www.familius.com

Our website is a different kind of place. Get inspired, read articles, discover books, watch videos, connect with our family experts, download books and apps and audiobooks, and along the way, discover how values and happy family life go together.

Join Our Family

There are lots of ways to connect with us! Subscribe to our newsletters at www.familius.com to receive uplifting daily inspiration, essays from our Pater Familius, a free ebook every month, and the first word on special discounts and Familius news.

Become an Expert

Familius authors and other established writers interested in helping families be happy are invited to join our family and contribute online content. If you have something important to say on the family, join our expert community by applying at:

www.familius.com/apply-to-become-a-familius-expert

Get Bulk Discounts

If you feel a few friends and family might benefit from what you've read, let us know and we'll be happy to provide you with quantity discounts. Simply email us at specialorders@familius.com.

Website: www.familius.com

Facebook: www.facebook.com/paterfamilius

Twitter: @familiustalk, @paterfamilius1

Pinterest: www.pinterest.com/familius

The most important work you ever

do will be within the walls of your

own home.

CPSIA information can be obtained at www.ICGtesting.com
Printed in the USA
LVOW11s0831300415

436613LV00001B/2/P